PRESERVES AND JAMS

Rhubarb
Berry
Jam

Bounty
Books

Introduction

Few things reap such satisfying results as turning up the heat under a pan of freshly-picked fruits or vegetables. The delicious bubbling of strawberries as they transform into sweet, deep red jam, and the rows of newly bottled chutneys remind your tastebuds of the real flavours of summer.

This paperback edition published in 2011 by Bounty Books,
a division of Octopus Publishing Group Limited,
Endeavour House, 189 Shaftesbury Avenue, London WC2H 8JY
www.octopusbooks.co.uk

An Hachette UK Company
www.hachette.co.uk

ISBN: 978-0-753722-05-3

Printed and bound in China

contents

Here are some tried-and-tested tips that will give you success every time; they are simple techniques that work perfectly, and it's important to read them before you start to cook. If you follow these procedures, your jams, jellies, pickles and chutneys will be a guaranteed triumph – tasty, delicious and simple to prepare

JAMS AND CONSERVES

Jam is based on either one fruit or several different fruits. The fruit is cooked until tender, until it will jell or become thick enough to spread when it is served at room temperature.

A conserve is a preserve made from whole or large pieces of fruit. It is made in the same way as jam.

fruit for jams and conserves

Fruit should be as freshly picked as possible, and slightly under-ripe; at this stage the pectin (the setting agent in preserves) content is at its highest. For best results in jam making, make small amounts at a time. The shorter cooking time will give better results in flavour, texture and appearance. As a guide, avoid using more than 2kg fruit for any jam recipe.

The most suitable fruits for jam making are those which have a good balance of acid and pectin; however, lemon juice contains both pectin and acid, and can be added to fruits low in acid or pectin to improve the setting properties of the jam.

■ Fruits with good balance of acid and pectin are: grapes, crab apples, currants, quinces, sour gooseberries, grapefruit, lemons, limes, sour apples, sour guavas, sour oranges, sour plums.

■ Fruits high in pectin and low in acid are: sweet apples, sweet guavas, sweet quinces. When making jam or jelly from these particular fruits, you need to add 2 tablespoons lemon juice to each 1kg fruit to increase the acid content.

■ Fruits low in pectin and high in acid are: apricots, pineapples, rhubarb, sour peaches. When making jam from these particular fruits, you need to add 2 tablespoons lemon juice to each 1kg fruit to increase the pectin content.

■ Fruits low in acid and pectin and not suitable without the addition of other fruits or juice for making jam are: pears, melons, sweet peaches, cherries and most berries including strawberries, raspberries and blueberries.

equipment used for preserves

Use large wide-topped stainless steel or enamel saucepans or boilers; do not use copper or unsealed cast iron pans because the acid in the preserve will damage the metal, and colour and flavour the ingredients. Aluminium pans should not be used as they can taint the flavour of the jam.

jam making

There is a basic method for making jam if you can't find a suitable recipe. This will always work provided the fruit is at its peak for jam making and the pectin/acid content is balanced.

1 Wash fruit well, cut away any bruised or damaged parts. Chop or slice fruit, reserve seeds; these provide extra pectin for setting.

They can be soaked separately in a cup half full of water, then the seeds strained out and discarded. The gelatinous liquid left is added to the fruit. Seeds can also be tied in a muslin bag and cooked with the fruit; the bag is discarded later.

Citrus rind needs overnight soaking to soften; in this case fruit is cooked in the soaking liquid – see details for marmalades, page 7.

2 Place fruit in pan; fruit layer should not be more than about 3cm deep (this allows rapid evaporation of liquid later). Add enough water to barely cover the fruit, cover pan, bring to boil over high heat, reduce heat, simmer gently to extract the pectin, acid and full flavour from the fruit. It is important that fruit be simmered until it is as tender as required; once the sugar is added, further cooking will not tenderise the fruit any more. This can take from about 10 minutes for soft fruit such as berries, or up to 1½ hours for tough citrus rinds.

3 Once the fruit or rind is tender, measure fruit mixture in a measuring cup or jug, allow 1 cup sugar to each cup of fruit mixture.

4 Return fruit mixture to pan; it should not be more than about 3cm deep; bring to boil. Add sugar to pan: the mixture at this stage should not be more than about 5cm deep.

5 Stir fruit mixture over high heat to dissolve sugar quickly. Sugar must be dissolved before mixture boils or jam may crystallise. Use pastry brush dipped in water to brush down sides of pan and wooden spoon to remove every single grain of sugar.

6 Once sugar is dissolved, boil the jam as rapidly as possible for minimum time given in recipe or until the mixture is thick or will jell. The time to jell can be some time between 10 minutes or up to an hour. Do not stir jam after sugar has dissolved, but use a wooden spoon to check that the jam is not sticking on the base of the pan, particularly towards the end of cooking time when jam is thicker. When jam has cooked for the required time, start testing to see if jam has jelled.

Dip a wooden spoon into the mixture, hold spoon up above mixture and tilt the bowl of the spoon towards you; as mixture cooks and thickens, the drops will fall more heavily from the spoon. When it is ready, 2 or 3 drops will roll down the edge of the spoon and join together in a heavy mass.

When this happens, remove jam or jelly from heat to stop further cooking. Drop a teaspoon of mixture onto a saucer which has been chilled in freezer for a few minutes, return saucer to freezer until jam or jelly is at room or serving temperature but not frozen.

■ Jam which has pieces of fruit in it should have formed a skin which wrinkles when pushed with the finger.

■ Jam which is pulpy in texture should be of a spreadable consistency.

■ Jelly should be a firm mass on the saucer. If mixture does not jell, return to the heat, boil rapidly until mixture will jell when tested; this may take only a few more minutes.

NOTE Jams and jellies will reach jelling point at 105°C to 106°C (220°F to 222°F). Any sugar thermometer can be used.

7 When jam is at jelling stage, skim surface, if necessary. If jam contains pieces of fruit, let it stand for 5 to 10 minutes (depending on the size and type of fruit used) before bottling. This allows the mixture to cool slightly and the fruit to disperse itself more evenly.

■ Marmalade usually requires the full 10 minutes standing time.

■ Jams made from pulpy fruit should be bottled immediately.

8 Pour jam into hot sterilised jars right to the top of the jar, jam will shrink on cooling.

9 Seal jars while hot. Label jam and store in a cool dark place. If jam has been cooked and sealed correctly, it will keep for at least 12 months. Once opened, store in refrigerator.

IF JAM HAS NOT SET

This is due to an imbalance of pectin and acid; or insufficient evaporation in the cooking process. Lemon juice can be added and jam re-boiled until it will jell when tested.

However, if jam has darkened in colour and has a caramel taste (which happens when sugar is overcooked) it cannot be re-boiled.

If the flavour is still palatable, commercial pectin (available in powdered or liquid form from health food stores and supermarkets) will set the jam; follow the manufacturer's directions.

JELLIES

A good jelly should be clear and translucent, firm enough to hold its own shape, but soft enough to quiver when cut with a spoon. The strained juice from the cooked fruit is combined with sugar, then cooked to a point at which it will set when cold. For information about fruit and equipment for jelly making, see under Jams and Conserves.

basic steps in jelly making

1 Wash fruit thoroughly, cut away any bruised or damaged parts. Chop fruit roughly, stems, seeds, skin and all.

2 Place prepared fruit in pan: fruit layer should not be more than 3cm deep. Add enough water to barely cover fruit, so fruit just begins to float.

3 Cover pan, bring to boil over high heat, reduce heat, simmer gently, covered, until fruit is tender and just beginning to become pulpy. The time varies, depending on type and ripeness of fruit, between 30 minutes and 1 hour.

4 Strain fruit mixture through a fine cloth. There are several easy methods of doing this:

■ A cone-shaped jelly bag with attachments for hanging can be bought from specialist kitchen stores (pictured right); have it thoroughly damp before use.

Place a large bowl under the bag or cloth. Pour the fruit and its liquid into the bag; do not push or force the fruit through, as this will cause the jelly to be cloudy. Cover the fruit loosely with greaseproof paper or tea towel to protect from dust and insects, leave liquid to drip through cloth; this will take up to 12 hours.

■ If you don't have a jelly straining kit, a jelly bag can be made by turning a chair or stool upside down on a table; tie corners of a square of damp fine cloth securely to the legs of the chair; leave cloth loose enough to dip in the centre.

■ If you are in a hurry, and not too concerned about the clarity of the jelly, the easiest, quickest

TO TEST FOR PECTIN CONTENT

Place 1 teaspoon of the strained fruit liquid in a glass, add 3 teaspoons methylated spirits; stir mixture gently with a teaspoon. We coloured about 1 tablespoon of the fruit liquid so it would show up clearly in the photograph. The liquid is normally almost colourless.

■ If mixture forms a fairly solid single jelly-like clot, the fruit liquid is high in pectin; in this case measure the liquid and use 1 cup sugar to each cup of liquid. (This jelly

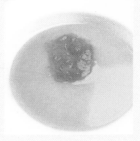

will set quickly, without long cooking time; there will be little evaporation of liquid, giving a good yield of jelly for the amount of fruit used.)

■ If several smaller clots of jelly form, the jelly is not high in pectin; use ¾ cup sugar to each cup fruit liquid.

■ If pectin test fails to produce any clots, or gives a mass of tiny clots, it will then be necessary to add some fruit juice naturally rich in pectin, usually 2 tablespoons fresh strained lemon juice to each 1kg fruit; add this after the sugar is dissolved.

way to strain fruit is through a large strainer or colander suspended over a bowl. Pour fruit mixture into strainer, press fruit with a wooden spoon to extract as much liquid as possible; discard the fruit pulp. To remove any remaining pulp from liquid, place a clean piece of damp fine cloth inside a strainer over a deep bowl, pour the liquid into cloth and allow it to drip through; do not force the liquid through the cloth.

5 Measure the liquid in a measuring cup or jug; determine how much sugar is required, according to recipes (generally ¾ cup or 1 cup sugar to each cup of liquid, depending on the pectin content of the fruit). If not following a recipe, the pectin test on page 6 will indicate the amount of sugar required.

6 Return fruit liquid to pan, there should not be more than 3cm covering base of pan.

7 Bring fruit liquid to the boil over high heat, add sugar, stir without boiling until sugar is dissolved; do not allow mixture to boil until sugar is dissolved or mixture may crystallise. All sugar grains must be brushed from sides of pan and from wooden spoon; use a pastry brush dipped in water to do this. Heat must be kept high to dissolve sugar quickly for best results.

8 When mixture comes to the boil, leave on high heat. Boil as rapidly as possible, uncovered, without stirring, for minimum time suggested in individual recipes. (These times are only a guide, as every batch of jelly will reach jelling point at a different time depending on ripeness of fruit; constant watching and testing is necessary.) See Jams and Conserves.

9 Jelly should foam up high in the pan, and high heat must be maintained without allowing the mixture to boil over. (This explains the need for a large pan.)

10 When mixture jells, allow bubbles to subside, lift off any scum which has appeared on the surface (it is wasteful to remove scum during cooking time). Use a jug to pour jelly in a slow, steady stream down the side of hot sterilised jars. Work quickly or jelly will set in pan. Do not stir or move the jelly too much with the jug, or jelly will not be clear.

11 Fill jars right to the top; jelly will shrink slightly on cooling.

12 Seal jars while hot. It will take at least 12 hours for jelly to become cold. Label and date jars, store in a cool dark place. Jelly should keep for 12 months. Once a jar is opened, keep refrigerated.

IF JELLY HAS NOT SET

This is due to a lack of pectin and/or acid. Re-boiling will cause the jelly to lose its clarity and texture; the addition of commercial pectin will also spoil its appearance, but will at least make the jelly set; follow manufacturer's directions. If all else fails, jellies can be set by using commercial jelly crystals. These jellies need to be stored in the refrigerator and will not keep long term.

Choose a similar flavour and colour to the home-made jelly, place the jelly crystals in a saucepan with 500ml water, stir over low heat until dissolved: do not boil. Add the unset home-made jelly and stir over low heat until any lumps are melted. The amount of jelly crystals required will, of course, depend on the consistency and quantity of the home-made jelly. As a guide, one 85g packet of jelly crystals should set about 1.5 litres home-made jelly.

MARMALADES

Marmalade is a clear jelly preserve with small pieces of rind or thin slices of fruit suspended in it. Marmalades are made from citrus fruits, or a combination of fruits, one or two being citrus. The name is said to have come from the Portuguese word for quince, marmelo.

Many marmalade recipes suggest fruit be sliced thinly, water added, and fruit soaked overnight. This extracts pectin and begins the process of softening the rind. If time does not permit overnight soaking, simply cook for longer than recipe instructs, but be careful not to evaporate an excessive amount of liquid or the balance of ingredients will be upset. Do not soak fruit in aluminium, cast iron or copper pans.

Some recipes require the seeds to be soaked and then boiled with the fruit; seeds are rich in pectin. (See rules for Jams and Conserves.)

Fruit, along with the water in which it was soaked, is cooked, covered, over a low heat until the rind becomes tender; this will take somewhere between 30 minutes and 1½ hours, depending on thickness and toughness of rind. Once sugar is added, further cooking will not tenderise the rind, so be sure rind is as tender as desired before the sugar is added. Follow detailed instructions for jam making when making marmalades; fruit can also be minced, blanched or chopped in a food processor.

JARS, STERILISING, SEALING AND STORAGE

JARS Jars must be glass, without chips or cracks; and should be sterilised. As a general rule, hot preserves go into hot sterilised jars, cold preserves go into cold sterilised jars. Jars must always be dry. Tea-towels and your hands must be clean when handling jars. Unclean jars can cause deterioration in all preserves.

TO STERILISE JARS In dishwasher, use rinse cycle and hottest temperature, do not use detergent.

Without a dishwasher:

Method 1: Place clean jars lying down in pan, cover completely with cold water, cover pan, bring to boil and boil, covered, for 20 minutes; carefully remove jars from water (thick rubber gloves and tongs are useful for this): drain well, stand right way up on wooden board. The heat from the jars will quickly evaporate any water remaining in the jars.

Method 2: Wash jars well in hot soapy water, rinse thoroughly in hot water to remove soap. Stand jars right way up on board in cold oven (do not allow jars to touch); turn oven to very slow, leave for 30 minutes, remove jars from oven.

TO SEAL JARS Preserve must be correctly sealed while it is still hot to prevent deterioration. Ordinary metal lids are not suitable; the acid content of the preserve will corrode the lids and the contents will be inedible. Special lined and treated or lacquered lids are suitable for sealing. Plastic screw-top lids give a good seal (plastic snap-on lids are not airtight enough). Plastic lids must be well washed, rinsed and dried. Some older preserving jars have glass lids; these can be sterilised by either of the above methods. Do not use aluminium foil, cellophane or paper covers for preserves; foil will be corroded by the acid in the preserves and paper and cellophane are not airtight enough for long term keeping. Wipe sealed jars clean, label and date.

STORAGE Store preserves in a cool, airy, dark, dry place (light can cause deterioration) until required. Once opened, all preserves must be stored, covered, in the refrigerator.

CHUTNEYS, PICKLES, RELISHES & SAUCES

These are all condiments made from vegetables, fruits, sugar, spices and vinegar. With these preserves, it is often necessary to secure whole spices in a muslin bag to be cooked with the preserve. This bag is discarded later.

INGREDIENTS

VINEGAR Use a good-quality malt vinegar; cheap vinegars do not contain enough acetic acid to act as a preservative. Good vinegar contains at least 4 per cent acetic acid.

Follow the same rules for Jams and Conserves for which type of pan to use, condition of fresh produce and bottling, sealing and storing.

SUGAR Sugar is the ingredient that preserves these home-cooked products. The only difference is in the colour and how that colour affects the finished preserve.

■ White sugar is used for jams, jellies, conserves and marmalades. Crystal sugar (white table sugar), caster sugar (finer) and loaf sugar can all be used with the same results. Caster sugar will dissolve faster than the other 2 varieties. We have specified when to use caster sugar; other than that, use crystal sugar.

■ Brown and white sugars are used in chutneys, pickles, relishes, sauces, etc. Brown or black sugar simply gives a richer colour and flavour.

■ If you want to enter your jam or jelly into a competition and have it at its sparkling best, warming the sugar will help you achieve clarity. The theory is the faster the sugar is dissolved and the faster the jam or jelly reaches jelling point, the better looking the preserve will be.

■ To warm sugar, Spread sugar into a baking dish, it should not be more than about 3cm deep. Place dish into slow oven for about 10 minutes, stir the sugar occasionally to distribute the warmth evenly.

LEMON JUICE This is rich in pectin and acid, and can make or rescue a sweet preserve. See information on Jams and Conserves. Lime juice is just as rich in pectin and acid and can be substituted for lemon juice at any time.

BERRIES AND CURRANTS Freshly picked, slightly under-ripe perfect fruit is always the best; however, frozen fruit can be substituted. If you don't have scales it is handy to know that 250g berries will fill a 250ml measuring cup or jug.

APPLES We used Granny Smith apples throughout this book. Try to obtain apples which are as freshly picked as possible and preferably under-ripe. Apples which have been in cold storage will not give good results.

SUGAR-FREE PRESERVES

Throughout this book we have included some preserve recipes which do not contain sugar. Some contain artificial sweeteners. These recipes must be kept, covered, in the refrigerator for up to 4 weeks.

MICROWAVE COOKERY

We have not given instructions for microwave cookery in this book. However, jams, conserves, marmalades and jellies can all be cooked in a microwave oven. As a guide, use no more than 500g fruit at a time, follow the same method as in conventional recipes. Also remember there is minimal amount of evaporation with microwave cooking and most preserves depend on this at the last stages of cooking. Always use a large shallow container, cook, covered or uncovered as the recipes state, check constantly during the cooking time. The flavour and colour of microwave cooked preserves is excellent. The golden rule is keep checking the preserve as it cooks.

CHUTNEYS, PICKLES AND SAUCES can also be cooked in small quantities in the microwave but, as evaporation is a necessary part of the process, it is best to cook these preserves in the conventional way.

RELISHES are usually fine to microwave; the colour retention is excellent.

BUTTERS AND SPREADS can be cooked in a microwave but require careful monitoring during cooking as the butters must not boil and the spreads are thick and tend to overcook quickly. We prefer to cook butters and spreads conventionally.

jams, jellies & conserves

strawberry jam

1kg STRAWBERRIES, QUARTERED
1.1kg SUGAR
80ml WATER
125ml FRESH LEMON JUICE
60ml GRAND MARNIER

1   Combine strawberries, sugar, the water and juice in large saucepan; stir over heat, without boiling, until sugar dissolves.
2   Boil, uncovered, stirring occasionally, about 20 minutes or until jam jells when tested. Stir in liqueur.
3   Pour hot jam into hot sterilised jars; seal while hot.

MAKES ABOUT 1 LITRE

■ Start saving jars now, ready for the year-round pleasures of making jams and conserves. Choose fruit in season when it is most plentiful and cheap (or use a good crop from your own garden). Fresh stone fruit and berries give the best results, but frozen fruits are a fairly good substitute. Before you start, it's important to read our tips and techniques on pages 4 to 9.

sugar-free berry jam

1kg BERRIES (ANY BERRIES CAN BE USED)
60ml LEMON JUICE
2 TEASPOONS LIQUID SWEETENER
125ml CERTO APPLE PECTIN

1   Combine berries and juice in large saucepan. Bring to boil, simmer, covered, for about 15 minutes or until fruit is soft. Stir in liquid sweetener.
2   Bring to boil; boil, uncovered, for 10 minutes. Stir in pectin; boil for 30 seconds or until jam jells when tested.
3   Pour hot jam into hot sterilised jars; seal while hot.

MAKES ABOUT 750ml

strawberry liqueur conserve

250g STRAWBERRIES
220g SUGAR
2 TEASPOONS FINELY GRATED
LEMON RIND
2 TABLESPOONS FRESH LEMON
JUICE

LIQUEUR
500g STRAWBERRIES
110g SUGAR
125ml GIN

1 Place strawberries in medium saucepan with sugar, rind, juice and reserved strawberries from liqueur. Stir gently over heat, without boiling, until sugar dissolves.
2 Boil, uncovered, gently stirring, occasionally, about 10 minutes or until conserve sets to a spreading consistency when tested.
3 Pour hot conserve into hot sterilised jars; seal while hot.

LIQUEUR Combine strawberries in jar with sugar and gin; cover, stand 3 days. Shake jar gently several times a day. Remove strawberries from liquid; reserve strawberries. (Liquid can be used as a dessert sauce or served as a liqueur).

MAKES ABOUT 500ml

TIP Any berry can be used in frozen berry jam.

easy mixed fruit jam

2 MEDIUM LEMONS (280g)
1 MEDIUM APPLE (150g)
60ml FRESH LEMON JUICE
300g FROZEN RASPBERRIES, THAWED
250g STRAWBERRIES, HALVED
440g SUGAR

1 Peel rind thinly from lemons, avoiding white pith. Cut rind into very thin strips. Peel and core apple, cut into thin wedges.
2 Combine rind, apple, juice, berries and sugar in large saucepan; stir over heat, without boiling, until sugar dissolves.
3 Boil, uncovered, stirring occasionally, about 15 minutes or until jam jells when tested.
4 Pour hot jam into hot sterilised jars; seal while hot.

MAKES ABOUT 750ml

frozen raspberry jam

4 LARGE ORANGES (880g)
1kg FROZEN RASPBERRIES, THAWED
1kg SUGAR
2 TABLESPOONS CRÈME DE
FRAMBOISES LIQUEUR
6 TABLESPOONS SLIVERED
ALMONDS

1 Thickly peel oranges, cut into segments; reserve any juices, discard seeds. Combine berries, oranges, reserved juice and sugar in large saucepan, stir gently over low heat without boiling until sugar is dissolved.
2 Bring to boil, boil, uncovered without stirring for about 30 minutes or until jam jells when tested.
3 Stir in liqueur and almonds; stand 10 minutes before pouring into hot sterilised jars; seal while hot.

MAKES ABOUT 1 LITRE

mixed berry jam

400g FROZEN RASPBERRIES
300g FROZEN BLACKBERRIES
300g FROZEN BLUEBERRIES
500ml WATER
125ml FRESH LEMON JUICE
880g SUGAR, APPROXIMATELY

1 Combine berries with the water and juice in large saucepan;
bring to a boil. Reduce heat; simmer, uncovered, 20 minutes.
2 Add sugar; stir over heat, without boiling, until sugar dissolves.
3 Boil, uncovered, stirring occasionally, about 15 minutes or until
jam jells when tested.
4 Pour hot jam into hot sterilised jars; seal while hot.

MAKES ABOUT 1.5 LITRES

three berry jam

500g STRAWBERRIES HULLED
500g BLACKBERRIES
500g RASPBERRIES
1.25kg SUGAR
60ml LEMON JUICE

1 Combine berries in large saucepan, stir gently over low heat for
5 minutes.
2 Measure fruit mixture, allow 1 cup sugar to each cup of fruit
mixture. Return fruit mixture and sugar to pan; stir in juice. Stir over
heat, without boiling, until sugar is dissolved.
3 Bring to boil and boil, uncovered, without stirring, for about
20 minutes or until jam jells when tested.
4 Pour hot jam into hot sterilised jars; seal while hot.

MAKES ABOUT 1.25 LITRES

BLUEBERRIES In
recent years, blueberries
have become increasingly
popular due to their
health-giving properties.
Not only are blueberries
a rich source of fibre,
calcium and vitamins A
and C, but they have
more antioxidants than
most other fruit and
vegetables.

TIP When buying the liquid sweetener for this recipe, read the label carefully to ensure that it is sugar-free.

sugar-free pear & blueberry jam

500g BLUEBERRIES
2 SMALL PEARS (300g), PEELED, CHOPPED COARSELY
2 TABLESPOONS LEMON JUICE
2 TEASPOONS WHITE VINEGAR
2 TEASPOONS LIQUID SWEETENER
3 TABLESPOONS CERTO APPLE PECTIN
½ TEASPOON TARTARIC ACID

1   Combine blueberries, pears, juice and vinegar in large saucepan; bring to a boil. Reduce heat; simmer, covered, about 25 minutes or until fruit is soft.
2   Stir in remaining ingredients; boil, uncovered, stirring occasionally, about 5 minutes or until jam jells when tested.
3   Pour hot jam into hot sterilised jars; seal while hot.

MAKES ABOUT 375ml

blackberry & apple jam

4 LARGE APPLES (800g)
800g BLACKBERRIES
125ml WATER
1kg SUGAR, APPROXIMATELY

1   Peel, core and finely chop apples. Combine apples, berries and water in large saucepan. Bring to boil, simmer, covered, for 30 minutes until fruit is soft. Measure fruit mixture, allow ¾ cup sugar to each cup of fruit mixture. Return fruit mixture and sugar to pan, stir over heat, without boiling, until sugar is dissolved.
2   Bring to boil, boil, uncovered, without stirring, for 15 minutes or until jam jells when tested.
3   Pour hot jam into hot sterilised jars; seal while hot.

MAKES ABOUT 1.5 LITRES

TIP You will need about two passionfruit for this recipe.

blueberry & passionfruit jam

750g BLUEBERRIES
750ml WATER
550g SUGAR, APPROXIMATELY
60ml FRESH LEMON JUICE
2 TABLESPOONS PASSIONFRUIT PULP

1 Combine blueberries and water in large saucepan; bring to a boil. Reduce heat; simmer, uncovered, about 20 minutes or until blueberries are tender.
2 Measure fruit mixture, allow ¾ cup sugar to each cup of fruit mixture. Return fruit mixture with sugar and juice to pan; stir over heat, without boiling, until sugar dissolves. Boil, uncovered, stirring occasionally, about 20 minutes or until jam jells when tested.
3 Stir in passionfruit pulp; stand 5 minutes.
4 Pour hot jam into hot sterilised jars; seal while hot.

MAKES ABOUT 750ml

blueberry jam

500g BLUEBERRIES
1 TABLESPOON LEMON JUICE
1 TEASPOON WHITE VINEGAR
440g SUGAR

1 Combine blueberries, juice and vinegar in large saucepan, bring to boil; simmer covered for 15 minutes or until blueberries are soft.
2 Stir in sugar, stir over heat, without boiling, until sugar is dissolved. Bring to boil, boil, uncovered, without stirring for 15 minutes or until jam jells when tested.
3 Pour hot jam into hot sterilised jars; seal while hot.

MAKES ABOUT 500ml

berry liqueur jam

1kg BERRIES (ANY BERRIES CAN BE USED)
1kg SUGAR
250ml LEMON JUICE
3 TABLESPOONS COINTREAU

1 Combine berries, sugar and juice in a large saucepan, stir over heat, without boiling, until sugar is dissolved.
2 Bring to boil, boil, uncovered, without stirring, for 25 minutes or until jam jells when tested.
3 Stir in liqueur. Pour hot jam into hot sterilised jars; seal while hot.

MAKES ABOUT 1.25 LITRES

raspberry & peach jam

500g RASPBERRIES
300g PEACHES, PEELED, CHOPPED
330g SUGAR
2 TEASPOONS GRATED LEMON
RIND
60ml WATER
2 TABLESPOONS PORT

1 Combine berries, peaches, sugar, rind and water in a large
saucepan. Stir over heat, without boiling, until sugar is dissolved.
2 Bring to boil, boil, uncovered, without stirring, for 15 minutes
or until jam jells when tested. Stir in port.
3 Pour hot jam into hot sterilised jars; seal while hot.

MAKES ABOUT 750ml

raspberry & apple jam

3 LARGE APPLES (600g)
800g RASPBERRIES
180ml WATER
1kg SUGAR, APPROXIMATELY
80ml LEMON JUICE
60ml CRÈME DE FRAMBOISES
LIQUEUR

1 Peel, core and finely chop apples.
2 Combine apples, berries and water in large saucepan, bring to
boil, simmer covered, for 1 hour.
3 Measure fruit mixture, allow ¾ cup sugar to each cup of fruit
mixture. Return fruit mixture and sugar to pan, stir in juice, stir over
heat, without boiling, until sugar is dissolved.
4 Bring to boil, boil, uncovered, without stirring, for 15 minutes or
until jam jells when tested. Stir in liqueur.
5 Pour hot jam into hot sterilised jars; seal while hot.

MAKES ABOUT 1 LITRE

raspberry jam

1½kg RASPBERRIES
2 TABLESPOONS LEMON JUICE
1½kg SUGAR
1 TABLESPOON FRAMBOISE LIQUEUR

1 Combine berries and juice in large saucepan, stir gently over low
heat for 5 minutes or until raspberries are soft.
2 Stir in sugar over heat, without boiling, until sugar is dissolved.
Bring to boil, boil, uncovered, without stirring, for 10 minutes or until
jam jells when tested. Stir in liqueur.
3 Pour hot jam into hot sterilised jars; seal while hot.

MAKES ABOUT 1.5 LITRES

TIPS The darker the cherries, the deeper and richer the resulting jam will be.

■ If you are making large quantities of cherry jam, it may be worth investing in a cherry pitter, available at good kitchenware shops.

cherry redcurrant jam

500g CHERRIES
600g REDCURRANTS
80ml WATER
600g SUGAR, APPROXIMATELY

1 Halve cherries, remove stones. Remove stems from redcurrants. Combine cherries, redcurrants and water in large saucepan. Bring to boil, simmer, covered, for 25 minutes or until fruit is soft.
2 Measure fruit mixture, allow ¾ cup sugar to each cup of fruit mixture. Return fruit mixture and sugar to pan; stir over heat, without boiling, until sugar is dissolved.
3 Bring to boil, boil, uncovered, without stirring, for 15 minutes or until jam jells when tested.
4 Pour hot jam into hot sterilised jars; seal while hot.

MAKES ABOUT 750ml

cherry & apple jam

2 LARGE APPLES (400g)
1kg CHERRIES
310ml WATER
80ml LEMON JUICE
1.25kg SUGAR, APPROXIMATELY

1 Peel, core and finely chop apples. Halve cherries, remove stones. Combine apples, cherries, water and juice in large saucepan. Bring to boil, simmer, covered, for about 15 minutes or until cherries are soft.
2 Measure fruit mixture, allow 1 cup sugar to each cup of fruit mixture. Return fruit mixture and sugar to pan; stir over heat, without boiling, until sugar is dissolved.
3 Bring to boil, boil, uncovered, without stirring, for about 30 minutes or until jam jells when tested.
4 Pour hot jam into hot sterilised jars; seal while hot.

MAKES ABOUT 1.25 LITRES

red plum jam

18 MEDIUM RED PLUMS (2kg)
1 LITRE WATER
80ml FRESH LEMON JUICE
1.3kg SUGAR

1 Cut plums into quarters, remove stones. Combine plums and the water in large saucepan; bring to a boil. Reduce heat; simmer, covered, 1 hour.
2 Add juice and sugar; stir over heat, without boiling, until sugar dissolves.
3 Boil, uncovered, stirring occasionally, about 20 minutes or until jam jells when tested.
4 Pour hot jam into hot sterilised jars; seal while hot.

MAKES ABOUT 2 LITRES

plum & apple jam

10 MEDIUM PLUMS (750g)
4 LARGE APPLES (800g)
1 TABLESPOON LEMON JUICE
875ml WATER
1kg SUGAR

1 Halve plums, reserve stones. Peel and finely chop apples, reserve seeds. Tie plum stones and apple seeds in piece of muslin.
2 Combine plums, apples, juice, water and muslin bag in large saucepan. Bring to boil, simmer, covered, without stirring, for 30 minutes or until fruit is soft. Discard muslin bag.
3 Stir in sugar over heat, without boiling, until sugar is dissolved. Bring to boil, boil uncovered, without stirring, for 30 minutes or until jam jells when tested.
4 Pour hot jam into hot sterilised jars; seal while hot.

MAKES ABOUT 1.25 LITRES

golden plum conserve

14 MEDIUM GOLDEN PLUMS (1kg)
250ml WATER
2 TABLESPOONS LEMON JUICE
60ml ORANGE JUICE
1.25kg SUGAR, APPROXIMATELY
240g SULTANAS
3 TABLESPOONS STEM GINGER, CHOPPED
1 TABLESPOON RUM

1 Halve plums, discard stones, cut plums into quarters.
2 Combine plums, water and juices in large saucepan. Bring to boil, simmer, covered, for about 10 minutes or until plums are soft.
3 Measure fruit mixture, allow 1 cup sugar to each cup of fruit mixture. Return fruit mixture and sugar to pan, stir over heat, without boiling, until sugar is dissolved. Stir in sultanas and ginger. Bring to boil, boil, uncovered, for about 20 minutes, without stirring, or until conserve jells when tested. Stir in rum.
4 Pour hot conserve into hot sterilised jars; seal while hot.

MAKES ABOUT 1.25 LITRES

TIP Although it is generally preferable to use fresh fruit when making jams and conserves, dried apricots add a delicious, rich flavour. You will find several recipes using dried apricots and other dried fruit on the next few pages.

fresh apricot jam

20 APRICOTS (1kg)
125ml WATER
60ml FRESH LEMON JUICE
1kg SUGAR

1   Halve apricots and remove stones. Combine apricots, the water and juice in large saucepan; bring to a boil. Reduce heat; simmer, covered, about 15 minutes or until apricots are tender.
2   Add sugar; stir over heat, without boiling, until sugar dissolves. Boil, uncovered, stirring occasionally, about 30 minutes or until jam jells when tested. Stand 5 minutes.
3   Pour hot jam into hot sterilised jars; seal while hot.

MAKES ABOUT 1.25 LITRES

apricot & apple jam

18 MEDIUM APRICOTS (750g)
5 LARGE APPLES (1kg), PEELED, CHOPPED
750ml WATER
1kg SUGAR, APPROXIMATELY

1   Halve apricots and discard stones. Combine apricots, apples and water in large saucepan.
2   Bring to boil, simmer, covered, for 30 minutes
3   Measure fruit mixture, allow ¾ cup sugar to each cup of fruit mixture. Return fruit mixture and sugar to pan, stir over heat, without boiling, until sugar is dissolved. Bring to boil, boil, uncovered, without stirring, for 30 minutes or until jam jells when tested.
4   Pour hot jam into hot sterilised jars; seal while hot.

MAKES ABOUT 1.5 LITRES

apricot & pineapple jam

25 MEDIUM APRICOTS (1kg)
1 SMALL PINEAPPLE (500g),
CHOPPED
125ml WATER
2 TABLESPOONS LEMON JUICE
660g SUGAR

1 Halve apricots, discard stones, cut apricots into quarters.
Combine apricots, pineapple, the water and juice in large saucepan.
2 Bring to boil, reduce heat, simmer, covered for 15 minutes or until
fruit is just soft. Stir in sugar, stir over heat, without boiling, until sugar
is dissolved. Bring to boil, boil, uncovered, without stirring, for about
15 minutes or until jam jells when tested.
3 Pour hot jam into hot sterilised jars; seal while hot.

MAKES ABOUT 1 LITRE

apricot & mandarin jam

4 MEDIUM MANDARINS (800g)
1 MEDIUM LEMON (140g)
250g DRIED APRICOTS, CHOPPED
COARSELY
1.25 LITRES WATER
1.5kg SUGAR, APPROXIMATELY

1 Peel rind from mandarins and lemon, taking care not to remove
any white pith with the rind. Shred rind finely. Discard membranes
from mandarins and lemon; chop flesh coarsely, discarding seeds.
2 Place rind, citrus flesh, apricots and the water in large saucepan;
bring to a boil. Reduce heat; simmer, covered, about 45 minutes or
until rind is transparent.
3 Measure fruit mixture, allow 1 cup sugar to each cup of fruit
mixture. Return fruit mixture with sugar to pan; stir over heat, without boiling, until sugar dissolves. Boil, uncovered, stirring occasionally,
about 10 minutes or until jam jells when tested.
4 Pour hot jam into hot sterilised jars; seal while hot.

MAKES ABOUT 1.75 LITRES

dried apricot jam

500g DRIED APRICOTS, CHOPPED
COARSELY
1.25 LITRES WATER
1kg SUGAR
60ml FRESH LEMON JUICE

1 Combine apricots and the water in large bowl; cover, stand overnight.
2 Transfer apricot mixture with sugar and juice to large saucepan; stir over heat, without boiling, until sugar dissolves. Boil, uncovered, stirring occasionally, about 25 minutes or until jam jells when tested.
3 Pour hot jam into hot sterilised jars; seal while hot.

MAKES ABOUT 1.5 LITRES

apricot amaretto jam

250g DRIED APRICOTS, SLICED
THINLY
375ml WATER
2 TEASPOONS FINELY GRATED
ORANGE RIND
250ml FRESH ORANGE JUICE
2 TABLESPOONS FRESH LEMON
JUICE
275g SUGAR
70g SLIVERED ALMONDS
2 TABLESPOONS AMARETTO

1 Place apricots and the water in medium bowl; cover, stand overnight.
2 Combine apricot mixture and rind in large saucepan; bring to a boil. Reduce heat; simmer, uncovered, about 10 minutes or until apricots are soft. Add juices and sugar; stir over heat, without boiling, until sugar dissolves.
3 Boil, uncovered, stirring occasionally, about 30 minutes or until jam jells when tested. Stir in almonds and liqueur.
4 Pour hot jam into hot sterilised jars; seal while hot.

MAKES ABOUT 625ml

apricot rum conserve

500g DRIED APRICOTS, CHOPPED
1 LITRE WATER
80ml FRESH LEMON JUICE
1kg SUGAR
2 TABLESPOONS DARK RUM

1 Combine apricots, the water and juice in large saucepan; bring to a boil. Reduce heat; simmer, covered, about 30 minutes or until apricots are tender.
2 Add sugar; stir over heat, without boiling, until sugar dissolves. Boil, uncovered, stirring occasionally, about 15 minutes or until conserve jells when tested. Stir in rum.
3 Pour hot conserve into hot sterilised jars; seal while hot.

MAKES ABOUT 1.5 LITRES

dried peach, apple & brandy jam

150g DRIED APPLES, CHOPPED COARSELY
400g COARSELY CHOPPED DRIED PEACHES
1.25 LITRES WATER
1kg SUGAR
60ml FRESH LEMON JUICE
2 TABLESPOONS BRANDY

1 Combine fruit and the water in large bowl; cover, stand overnight.
2 Transfer fruit mixture with sugar and juice to large saucepan; stir over heat, without boiling, until sugar dissolves. Boil, uncovered, stirring occasionally, about 25 minutes or until jam jells when tested. Remove pan from heat; stir in brandy.
3 Pour hot jam into hot sterilised jars; seal while hot.

MAKES ABOUT 1.5 LITRES

TIP You will need about
eight passionfruit for the
peach & passionfruit recipe.

3 MEDIUM LEMONS (500g)
1 LARGE APPLE (200g), CHOPPED
2 CLOVES
10 MEDIUM PEACHES (1.5kg), PEELED
250ml WATER
½ TEASPOON GROUND ALLSPICE
660g SUGAR

peach jam

1 Using vegetable peeler, remove rind thinly from lemons. Squeeze juice from lemons; you will need 2 tablespoons juice. Tie lemon rind, apple and cloves in a double piece of muslin; secure with string. Halve peaches, remove stones, chop peaches.

2 Combine peaches, water, reserved lemon juice and muslin bag in large saucepan. Bring to boil, simmer, covered, for about 30 minutes until fruit is just soft. Discard muslin bag.

3 Stir allspice and sugar into pan; stir over heat, without boiling, until sugar is dissolved. Bring to boil, boil, uncovered, without stirring, for 15 minutes or until jam jells when tested.

4 Pour hot jam into hot sterilised jars; seal while hot.

MAKES ABOUT 750ml

peach & passionfruit jam

1 SMALL ORANGE (180g)
1 MEDIUM LEMON (140g)
2 TABLESPOONS WATER
500ml WATER, EXTRA
7 MEDIUM PEACHES (1kg), PEELED, THINLY SLICED
880g SUGAR, APPROXIMATELY
160ml PASSIONFRUIT PULP

1 Chop unpeeled orange and lemon coarsely, remove and reserve seeds. Put seeds and the 2 tablespoons of water in small bowl; cover, set aside. Blend or process orange and lemon mixture until finely chopped. Combine fruit mixture with extra water in large bowl. Stand both fruit mixture and seeds, separately, overnight.

2 Drain seeds over small bowl; reserve liquid, discard seeds. Combine seed liquid with fruit mixture in large saucepan; bring to a boil. Reduce heat; simmer, covered, about 25 minutes or until rind is tender. Stir in peaches; simmer, covered, about 20 minutes or until peaches are soft.

3 Measure fruit mixture, allow 1 cup sugar to each cup of fruit mixture. Return fruit mixture with sugar to pan; stir over heat, without boiling, until sugar dissolves. Boil, uncovered, stirring occasionally, about 15 minutes or until jam jells when tested. Stand 5 minutes; stir in passionfruit pulp.

4 Pour hot jam into hot sterilised jars; seal while hot.

MAKES ABOUT 1.25 LITRES

peach & ginger jam

10 MEDIUM PEACHES (1.5kg), PEELED
2 LARGE APPLES (400g), PEELED, CHOPPED
4 TABLESPOONS STEM GINGER, FINELY CHOPPED
2 TEASPOONS GRATED LEMON RIND
125ml LEMON JUICE
1.5kg SUGAR

1 Cut peaches in half, discard stones. Combine peaches, apples, ginger, rind and juice in large saucepan. Bring to boil; simmer, covered, for about 30 minutes or until fruit is soft.
2 Stir in sugar over heat, without boiling, until sugar is dissolved. Bring to boil, boil, uncovered, without stirring, for 15 minutes or until jam jells when tested.
3 Pour hot jam into hot sterilised jars; seal while hot.

MAKES ABOUT 2 LITRES

nectarine liqueur jam

8 LARGE NECTARINES (1.5kg)
125ml LEMON JUICE
440g SUGAR, APPROXIMATELY
2 TABLESPOONS AMARETTO

1 Halve nectarines, discard stones, finely chop nectarines. Combine nectarines and juice in large saucepan. Bring to boil, simmer, covered, for about 20 minutes or until nectarines are soft.
2 Measure fruit mixture, allow ¾ cup sugar to each cup of fruit mixture. Return fruit mixture and sugar to pan, stir over heat, without boiling, until sugar is dissolved. Bring to boil, boil, uncovered, without stirring, for 10 minutes or until jam jells when tested. Stir in the liqueur.
3 Pour hot jam into hot sterilised jars; seal while hot.

MAKES ABOUT 750ml

pear, ginger & lemon jam

5 MEDIUM LEMONS (900g)
6 MEDIUM PEARS (1kg), PEELED, CHOPPED
3 TABLESPOONS STEM GINGER, CHOPPED
1.25 LITRES WATER
1kg SUGAR

1 Slice unpeeled lemons, reserve seeds. Tie seeds in a piece of muslin. Combine lemons and any juice and bag of seeds with remaining ingredients in large saucepan, stir over heat, without boiling, until sugar is dissolved.
2 Bring to boil, simmer, uncovered, without stirring, for 1 hour or until jam jells when tested. Discard muslin bag.
3 Pour hot jam into hot sterilised jars; seal while hot.

MAKES ABOUT 1 LITRE

pear & pineapple jam

10 MEDIUM PEARS (1.5kg), PEELED, CHOPPED
1 LARGE PINEAPPLE (1.5kg), CHOPPED
1 TABLESPOON GRATED LEMON RIND
330ml LEMON JUICE
500ml WATER
1.5kg SUGAR

1 Combine pears with pineapple, rind, juice and water in a large saucepan. Bring to boil, simmer, uncovered, for about 45 minutes or until mixture is reduced by half.
2 Stir in sugar, stir over heat, without boiling, until sugar is dissolved. Bring to boil, boil, uncovered, without stirring, for 15 minutes or until jam jells when tested.
3 Pour hot jam into hot sterilised jars; seal while hot.

MAKES ABOUT 2 LITRES

pineapple jam

2 MEDIUM PINEAPPLES (2kg), PEELED, CORED, CHOPPED COARSELY
1.25 LITRES WATER
165ml FRESH LEMON JUICE
1.5kg SUGAR

1 Combine pineapples, the water and juice in large saucepan; bring to a boil. Reduce heat; simmer, covered, about 1 hour or until pineapple is soft.
2 Stir in sugar; stir over heat, without boiling, until sugar is dissolved. Boil, uncovered, without stirring, about 30 minutes or until jam jells when tested.
3 Pour hot jam into hot sterilised jars; seal while hot.

MAKES ABOUT 1.5 LITRES

tropical treat jam

5 LARGE APPLES (1kg)
3 MEDIUM PEARS (500g)
3 MEDIUM (500g) BANANAS, CHOPPED
1 SMALL PINEAPPLE (500g), CHOPPED
125ml LEMON JUICE
330ml ORANGE JUICE
1.5kg SUGAR
PULP FROM 3 PASSIONFRUIT

1 Peel, core and chop apples and pears. Tie apple and pear skins and the cores in a piece of muslin.
2 Combine apples, pears, bananas, pineapple, juices and muslin bag in large saucepan. Bring to boil; simmer, covered, for 20 minutes or until fruit is soft. Discard muslin bag.
3 Add sugar; stir over heat, without boiling, until sugar is dissolved. Bring to boil, boil, uncovered, without stirring, for 60 minutes or until jam jells when tested. Stir in passionfruit pulp, stand 5 minutes.
4 Pour hot jam into hot sterilised jars; seal while hot.

MAKES ABOUT 2 LITRES

fruit salad jam

250g DRIED APRICOTS
500ml WATER
250ml UNDRAINED CANNED CRUSHED PINEAPPLE IN SYRUP
125ml FRESH ORANGE JUICE
60ml PASSIONFRUIT PULP
660g SUGAR
300g SLICED BANANAS

1 Combine apricots and the water in medium bowl; cover; stand 3 hours or overnight.
2 Combine undrained apricots with pineapple in large saucepan; simmer, covered, 15 minutes. Add juice and passionfruit pulp, bring to a boil; reduce heat, simmer, covered, 10 minutes.
3 Add sugar; stir over heat, without boiling, until sugar dissolves.
4 Add banana; boil, uncovered, stirring occasionally, about 20 minutes or until jam jells when tested. Stand 5 minutes.
5 Pour hot jam into hot sterilised jars; seal while hot.

MAKES ABOUT 1.5 LITRES

TIP You will need three large bananas and about three passionfruit for this recipe.

TIP The green food colouring in this recipe gives the
jam a lush, green colour. If
you prefer not to use it, the
finished jam will taste just as
delicious!

kiwi fruit jam

12 LARGE KIWI FRUIT (1.2kg)
2 TABLESPOONS CERTO APPLE
PECTIN
2 TABLESPOONS WATER
2 TABLESPOONS FRESH LEMON JUICE
440g SUGAR
GREEN FOOD COLOURING,
OPTIONAL

1   Cut peeled kiwi fruit into eighths, discard seeds and core.
Blend or process the water, juice and 1 tablespoon of the sugar
until smooth. Add kiwi fruit; process until chopped coarsely.
2   Combine kiwi fruit mixture with remaining sugar in large
saucepan; stir over heat, without boiling, until sugar dissolves.
3   Boil, uncovered, stirring occasionally, 10 minutes. Stir in pectin;
boil for 30 seconds or until jam jells when tested.
4   Tint with food colouring, if desired.
5   Pour hot jam into hot sterilised jars; seal while hot.

MAKES ABOUT 625ml

nutty tropical fruit jam

2 MEDIUM MANGOES (500g)
CHOPPED
1 SMALL PAPAYA CHOPPED
80ml LEMON JUICE
660g SUGAR, APPROXIMATELY
6 TABLESPOONS PINE NUTS
1½ TABLESPOONS KIRSCH

1   Combine mangoes, papaya and juice in a large saucepan. Bring
to boil; simmer, covered, for 10 minutes or until fruit is soft.
2   Measure fruit mixture, allow 1 cup sugar to each cup of fruit
mixture. Return fruit mixture and sugar to pan. Stir over heat, without boiling, until sugar is dissolved.
3   Bring to boil, boil, uncovered, without stirring, for 15 minutes or
until jam jells when tested.
4   Stir in nuts and liqueur, stand for 10 minutes, stirring occasionally
until nuts remain suspended in jam.
5   Pour hot jam into hot sterilised jars; seal while hot.

MAKES ABOUT 750ml

fig & apple jam

3 LARGE APPLES (600g), PEELED, CHOPPED
1 LITRE WATER
6 MEDIUM FIGS (500g), CHOPPED
500ml WATER, EXTRA
1kg SUGAR, APROXIMATELY

1   Combine apples and water in large saucepan, bring to boil, simmer, covered, for about 30 minutes. Stir in figs and extra water, bring to boil, simmer, covered, for 10 minutes or until figs are soft.
2   Measure fruit mixture, allow ¾ cup sugar to each cup of fruit mixture. Return fruit mixture with sugar to pan; stir over heat, without boiling, until is sugar dissolved. Bring to boil, boil, uncovered, without stirring, for about 30 minutes or until jam jells when tested.
4   Pour hot jam into hot sterilised jars; seal while hot.

MAKES ABOUT 1.25 LITRES

papaya & pineapple jam

2 MEDIUM FIRM PAPAYAS (2kg)
1 MEDIUM PINEAPPLE (1.25kg)
100g FINELY CHOPPED STEM GINGER
500ml FRESH LEMON JUICE
2kg SUGAR

1   Quarter, deseed and peel papayas; chop into 2cm pieces. Peel pineapple, remove core; chop pineapple into 2cm pieces. Combine papaya, pineapple, ginger and juice in large saucepan; bring to a boil. Reduce heat; simmer, uncovered, 5 minutes.
2   Add sugar; stir over heat, without boiling, until sugar dissolves. Boil, uncovered, stirring occasionally, about 30 minutes or until jam jells when tested; stand 5 minutes.
3   Pour hot jam into hot sterilised jars; seal while hot.

MAKES ABOUT 3 LITRES

PAPAYA Also known as pawpaw, this large, pear-shaped red-orange tropical fruit has a fairly intense flavour. The seeds, which are edible, have a peppery taste.

TIP Rhubarb is a vegetable (though eaten as a fruit) with cherry-red stalks and green leaves. The stalks are the only edible part of rhubarb; the leaves contain oxalic acid and are toxic.

rhubarb & apple jam

500g FINELY CHOPPED RHUBARB
5 LARGE APPLES (1kg), PEELED, SLICED THINLY
125ml WATER
125ml FRESH LEMON JUICE
1kg SUGAR, APPROXIMATELY

1   Combine rhubarb, apple, the water and juice in large saucepan; bring to a boil. Reduce heat; simmer, covered, about 20 minutes or until fruit is pulpy.
2   Measure fruit mixture, allow ¾ cup sugar to each cup of fruit mixture. Return fruit mixture with sugar to pan; stir over heat, without boiling, until sugar dissolves. Boil, uncovered, stirring occasionally, about 10 minutes or until jam sets to a spreading consistency when tested.
3   Pour hot jam into hot sterilised jars; seal while hot.

MAKES ABOUT 1.5 LITRES

rhubarb & ginger jam

1.5kg RHUBARB CHOPPED
250ml WATER
2 TABLESPOONS LEMON JUICE
5cm PIECE FRESH GINGER, PEELED
1.25kg CASTER SUGAR
6 TABLESPOONS FINELY CHOPPED STEM GINGER

1   Combine rhubarb, water, juice and fresh ginger in large saucepan. Bring to boil, simmer, covered for 1 hour. Remove and discard ginger.
2   Measure fruit mixture, allow ¾ cup sugar to each cup of fruit mixture. Return fruit mixture and sugar to pan. Stir over heat, without boiling, until sugar is dissolved. Stir in stem ginger.
3   Bring to boil, boil, uncovered, without stirring, for 15 minutes or until jam jells when tested.
4   Pour hot jam into hot sterilised jars; seal while hot.

MAKES ABOUT 1.5 LITRES

TIP Dark plums will give a
great colour to this jelly.

plum jelly

2kg PLUMS
1 LITRE WATER
80ml LEMON JUICE
660g SUGAR, APPROXIMATELY

1   Combine plums, water and juice in large saucepan. Bring to boil simmer, covered, for 10 minutes or until plums are soft.
2   Strain mixture through fine cloth. Allow mixture to drip through cloth slowly, do not squeeze cloth; discard pulp.
3   Measure liquid, pour into large saucepan. Add correct amount of sugar (according to pectin test, page 6) to each cup of liquid, stir over heat, without boiling, until sugar is dissolved.
4   Bring to boil, boil, uncovered, for 15 minutes or until jelly sets when tested.
5   Pour hot jelly into hot sterilised jars; seal while hot.

MAKES ABOUT 750ml

raspberry jelly

2kg RASPBERRIES
1kg SUGAR, APPROXIMATELY
1 TABLESPOON LEMON JUICE

1   Place raspberries in large pan, stir over low heat for 10 minutes or until pulpy. Strain mixture through fine cloth. Allow liquid to drip through cloth slowly, do not squeeze cloth; discard pulp.
2   Measure liquid, pour into large saucepan. Add correct amount of sugar (according to pectin test, page 6) to each cup of liquid, add juice, stir over heat, without boiling, until sugar is dissolved.
3   Bring to boil, boil, uncovered, for 10 minutes or until jelly sets when tested.
4   Pour hot jelly into hot sterilised jars; seal while hot.

MAKES ABOUT 1 LITRE

JELLIES The good thing about making jelly is that you do minimal preparation. Just chop the unpeeled fruit and use the lot – skins, cores and all! Each jelly will need a simple pectin test to determine how much sugar to add (see tips & techniques pages 6–7).

TIP Jelly must be slowly strained through a jelly bag or fine cloth. See pages 6–7 for further details.

redcurrant jelly

1.5kg REDCURRANTS
1.5 LITRES WATER
1 TEASPOON FRESH LEMON JUICE
550g SUGAR, APPROXIMATELY
1 TABLESPOON GRAND MARNIER

1   Combine redcurrants, the water and juice in large saucepan; bring to a boil. Reduce heat; simmer, covered, about 30 minutes or until redcurrants are soft.
2   Strain mixture through large piece of damp muslin into large bowl; allow mixture to drip through cloth for several hours or over-night. Do not squeeze or press the mixture through cloth.
3   Measure the strained liquid, discard pulp. Allow the correct amount of sugar (according to pectin test, page 6) to each cup of liquid. Return liquid with sugar to clean large saucepan; stir over heat, without boiling, until sugar dissolves. Boil, uncovered, without stirring, about 15 minutes or until jelly sets when tested. Stir in liqueur.
4   Pour hot jelly into hot sterilised jars; seal while hot.

MAKES ABOUT 750ml

redcurrant & raspberry jelly

600g REDCURRANTS
800g RASPBERRIES
250ml WATER
440g SUGAR, APPROXIMATELY

1   Combine fruit and water in large saucepan. Bring to boil simmer, covered, for 25 minutes or until fruit is soft.
2   Strain mixture through fine cloth. Allow liquid to drip through cloth slowly, do not squeeze cloth; discard pulp.
3   Measure liquid, pour into large saucepan. Add correct amount of sugar (according to pectin test, page 6) to each cup of liquid, stir over heat, without boiling, until sugar is dissolved. Bring to boil, boil, uncovered, for 10 minutes or until jelly sets when tested.
4   Pour hot jelly into hot sterilised jars; seal while hot.

MAKES ABOUT 500ml

grape jelly

1.5kg BLACK GRAPES
165ml WATER
80ml LEMON JUICE
500g SUGAR, APPROXIMATELY
3 TABLESPOONS CERTO APPLE PECTIN

1 Using scissors, snip grapes from main stems, leaving small stems attached to grapes. Crush grapes in large pan, stir in water and juice.
2 Bring to boil, simmer, covered, for 10 minutes or until fruit is pulpy. Strain mixture through fine cloth. Allow mixture to drip through cloth slowly, do not squeeze cloth, discard pulp.
3 Measure liquid, pour into large saucepan. Add correct amount of sugar (according to pectin test, page 6) to each cup of liquid. Stir over heat, without boiling, until sugar is dissolved. Bring to boil, stir in pectin, boil, uncovered, for 5 minutes or until jelly sets when tested.
4 Pour hot jelly into hot sterilised jars; seal while hot.

MAKES ABOUT 750ml

grape & sherry jelly

1kg WHITE GRAPES, CRUSHED
1 MEDIUM LEMON (140g), SLICED THINLY
2 LARGE APPLES (400g), CHOPPED COARSELY
125ml SWEET WHITE WINE
180ml WATER
1 CINNAMON STICK
4 CARDAMOM SEEDS, CRUSHED
385g SUGAR, APPROXIMATELY
2 TABLESPOONS SWEET SHERRY

1 Combine grapes, lemon and apple (including seeds and cores) with wine, the water, cinnamon and cardamom in large saucepan; bring to a boil. Reduce heat; simmer, covered, 1 hour.
2 Strain mixture through large piece of damp muslin into large bowl; allow mixture to drip through cloth for several hours or overnight. Do not squeeze or press the mixture through the cloth.
3 Measure the strained liquid, discard pulp. Allow the correct amount of sugar (according to pectin test, page 6) to each cup of liquid. Return liquid with sugar to clean large saucepan; stir over heat, without boiling, until sugar dissolves. Boil, uncovered, without stirring, about 10 minutes or until jelly sets when tested. Stir in sherry.
4 Pour hot jelly into hot sterilised jars; seal while hot.

MAKES ABOUT 500ml

TIPS Choose the grapes for your jelly with care. Some seedless white grapes, for example, have little flavour. Seedless or with seeds doesn't matter, as straining will remove them.

black grape & port jelly

1kg BLACK GRAPES
2 MEDIUM LEMONS (280g),
CHOPPED COARSELY
1 LITRE WATER
125ml PORT
1kg SUGAR, APPROXIMATELY

1 Combine grapes, lemon (including rind and seeds) and the water in large saucepan; bring to a boil. Reduce heat; simmer, covered, 45 minutes. Stir in port, crush grapes in pan using a potato masher.
2 Simmer, covered, 45 minutes. Strain mixture through large piece of damp muslin into large bowl; allow mixture to drip through cloth for several hours or overnight. Do not squeeze or press the mixture through the cloth as this will result in cloudy jelly.
3 Measure the strained liquid, discard pulp. Allow the correct amount of sugar (according to pectin test, page 6) to each cup of liquid. Return liquid with sugar to clean large saucepan; stir over heat, without boiling, until sugar dissolves. Boil, uncovered, without stirring, about 15 minutes or until jelly sets when tested.
4 Pour hot jelly into hot sterilised jars; seal while hot.

MAKES ABOUT 1 LITRE

quince jelly

1.75kg QUINCES, CHOPPED
1.75 LITRES WATER
1.25kg SUGAR, APPROXIMATELY
125ml LEMON JUICE

1 Combine quinces and water in large saucepan, bring to boil, simmer, covered, for 1 hour or until quinces are soft.
2 Strain mixture through fine cloth. Allow liquid to drip through cloth slowly, do not squeeze cloth; discard pulp.
3 Measure liquid, pour into large saucepan. Add correct amount of sugar (according to pectin test, page 6) to each cup of liquid, add juice, stir over heat, without boiling, until sugar is dissolved.
4 Bring to boil, boil, uncovered, for 25 minutes or until jelly sets when tested. Pour hot jelly into hot sterilised jars; seal while hot.

MAKES ABOUT 1 LITRE

TIP You will need about six
passionfruit for this recipe.

apple passionfruit jelly

5 LARGE APPLES (1kg)
1.5 LITRES WATER
1kg SUGAR, APPROXIMATELY
125ml PASSIONFRUIT PULP

1 Cut unpeeled apples crossways into thin slices. Combine apples
(including seeds and cores) with the water in large saucepan; bring
to a boil. Reduce heat; simmer, covered, 1 hour.
2 Strain mixture through large piece of damp muslin into large
bowl; allow mixture to drip through cloth for several hours or
overnight. Do not squeeze or press the mixture through the cloth
as this will result in cloudy jelly.
3 Measure the strained liquid, discard pulp. Allow the correct
amount of sugar (according to pectin test, page 6) to each cup of
liquid. Return liquid with sugar to clean large saucepan; stir over
heat, without boiling, until sugar dissolves. Boil, uncovered, without
stirring, about 15 minutes or until jelly sets when tested. Gently stir
passionfruit pulp through jelly; stand 5 minutes.
4 Pour hot jelly into hot sterilised jars; seal while hot.

MAKES ABOUT 875ml

apple jelly

1kg APPLES CHOPPED
1.5 LITRES WATER
1kg SUGAR, APPROXIMATELY

1 Combine apples and water in large saucepan. Bring to boil,
simmer, covered, for 1 hour.
2 Strain mixture through fine cloth. Allow liquid to drip through
cloth slowly, do not squeeze cloth; discard pulp.
3 Measure liquid, pour into large saucepan. Add correct amount
of sugar (according to pectin test, page 6) to each cup of liquid, stir
over heat, without boiling, until sugar is dissolved. Bring to boil, boil,
uncovered, for 15 minutes or until jelly sets when tested.
4 Pour hot jelly into hot sterilised jars; seal while hot.

MAKES ABOUT 750ml

apple & rosé jelly

5 LARGE APPLES (1kg)
1 MEDIUM LEMON (140g)
1.5 LITRES WATER
250ml ROSÉ WINE
1.5kg SUGAR, APPROXIMATELY

1   Chop unpeeled apples and lemon coarsely. Combine chopped fruit (including seeds and cores) with the water in large saucepan; bring to a boil. Reduce heat; simmer, covered, about 1 hour or until fruit is pulpy.

2   Add wine; simmer, covered, 30 minutes. Strain mixture through large piece of damp muslin into large bowl; allow mixture to drip through cloth for several hours or overnight. Do not squeeze or press the mixture through the cloth as this will result in cloudy jelly.

3   Measure the strained liquid, discard pulp. Allow the correct amount of sugar (according to pectin test, page 6) to each cup of liquid. Return liquid with sugar to clean large saucepan; stir over heat, without boiling, until sugar dissolves. Boil, uncovered, without stirring, about 10 minutes or until jelly sets when tested.

4   Pour hot jelly into hot sterilised jars; seal while hot.

MAKES ABOUT 1.5 LITRES

TIP We have used Granny Smith apples throughout this book. Try to obtain apples which are as freshly picked as possible and preferably under-ripe. Apples which have been in cold storage will not give good results.

jams, jellies &
conserves

blackberry, apple & mint jelly

400g APPLES, CHOPPED
1 MEDIUM LEMON, CHOPPED
750g BLACKBERRIES
1 LITRE WATER
3 TABLESPOONS CHOPPED FRESH MINT
440g SUGAR, APPROXIMATELY
½ TEASPOON CHOPPED FRESH MINT, EXTRA

1 Combine apples, lemon, blackberries, water and mint in large saucepan. Bring to boil simmer, covered, for 1 hour.
2 Strain mixture through fine cloth. Allow liquid to drip through cloth slowly, do not squeeze cloth; discard pulp.
3 Measure liquid, pour into large saucepan. Add correct amount of sugar (according to pectin test, page 6) to each cup of liquid, stir over heat, without boiling, until sugar is dissolved. Bring to boil, boil, uncovered for 10 minutes or until jelly sets when tested. Add extra mint.
4 Pour hot jelly into hot sterilised jars; seal while hot.

MAKES ABOUT 1 LITRE

honey sauternes jelly

5 LARGE APPLES (1kg), CHOPPED COARSELY
2 TABLESPOONS FRESH LEMON JUICE
500ml WATER
250ml SAUTERNES
60ml HONEY
660g SUGAR, APPROXIMATELY

1 Combine apple (including seeds and cores), juice, the water, wine and honey in large saucepan; bring to a boil. Reduce heat; simmer, covered, 1 hour.
2 Strain mixture through large piece of damp muslin into large bowl; allow mixture to drip through cloth for several hours or overnight. Do not squeeze or press the mixture through the cloth as this will result in cloudy jelly.
3 Measure the strained liquid, discard pulp. Allow the correct amount of sugar (according to pectin test, page 6) to each cup of liquid. Return liquid with sugar to clean large saucepan; stir over heat, without boiling, until sugar dissolves. Boil, uncovered, without stirring, about 10 minutes or until jelly sets when tested.
4 Pour hot jelly into hot sterilised jars; seal while hot.

MAKES ABOUT 750ml

TIP Any member of the tangerine family is suitable for this recipe – try clementines, mandarins or satsumas.

tangerine jelly

1kg TANGERINES, CHOPPED
1 MEDIUM LEMON, CHOPPED
2.5 LITRES WATER
550g SUGAR, APPROXIMATELY

1   Combine tangerines, lemon and water in large saucepan. Bring to boil, simmer, covered, for 1 hour or until fruit is soft and pulpy. Strain mixture through fine cloth. Allow liquid to drip through cloth slowly, do not squeeze cloth; discard pulp.
2   Measure liquid, pour into large saucepan. Add correct amount of sugar (according to pectin test, page 6) to each cup of liquid, stir over heat, without boiling, until sugar is dissolved.
3   Bring to boil, boil, uncovered, for 5 minutes or until jelly sets when tested. Pour hot jelly into hot sterilised jars; seal while hot.

MAKES ABOUT 500ml

guava jelly

1.5kg GUAVAS, CHOPPED
1 LITRE WATER
440g SUGAR, APPROXIMATELY
2 TABLESPOONS LIME JUICE

1   Combine guavas and water in large saucepan. Bring to boil; simmer, covered, for 25 minutes or until fruit is soft and pulpy. Strain mixture through fine cloth. Allow liquid to drip through cloth slowly, do not squeeze cloth; discard pulp.
2   Measure liquid, pour into large saucepan. Add correct amount of sugar (according to pectin test, page 6) to each cup of liquid, add juice, stir over heat, without boiling, until sugar is dissolved.
3   Bring to boil, boil, uncovered, for 15 minutes or until jelly sets when tested. Pour hot jelly into hot sterilised jars; seal while hot.

MAKES ABOUT 500ml

marmalades

whisky seville marmalade

4 MEDIUM SEVILLE ORANGES (1kg)
2 LITRES WATER
2.4kg SUGAR, APPROXIMATELY
60ml WHISKY

1 Slice unpeeled oranges very thinly; reserve seeds. Put seeds and 250ml water in small bowl; cover, set aside. Place fruit in large bowl with remaining water. Stand both fruit and seeds separately overnight.
2 Drain seeds over small bowl; reserve liquid, discard seeds. Combine fruit mixture and seed liquid in large pan; bring to a boil. Reduce heat; simmer, covered, about 1 hour or until rind is tender.
3 Measure fruit mixture, allow 1 cup sugar to each cup of fruit mixture. Return fruit mixture with sugar to pan; stir over heat, without boiling, until sugar dissolves. Boil, uncovered, stirring occasionally, about 30 minutes or until marmalade jells when tested. Stand 5 minutes, stir in whisky.
4 Pour hot marmalade into hot sterilised jars; seal while hot.

MAKES ABOUT 2.5 LITRES

■ Marmalades are jams which always include a citrus fruit and usually have rind suspended in the mixture. Citrus fruits are rich in pectin, so there is rarely any trouble getting marmalades to set. Be sure you read our tips & techniques on pages 4–9 before you start.

seville orange marmalade

6 SMALL SEVILLE ORANGES (1kg)
2 LITRES WATER
2kg SUGAR, APPROXIMATELY

1 Slice unpeeled oranges finely, reserve seeds. Combine oranges and the water in bowl, cover; stand overnight. Place seeds in a cup, barely cover with water, cover; stand overnight.
2 Transfer fruit mixture to large saucepan, bring to boil, simmer, covered for about 45 minutes or until rind is soft.
3 Measure fruit mixture, allow 1 cup sugar to each cup of fruit mixture. Return fruit and sugar to pan, stir in liquid from seeds; discard seeds. Stir over heat, without boiling, until sugar is dissolved.
4 Bring to boil, boil, uncovered, without stirring. for 20 minutes or until marmalade jells when tested.
5 Pour hot marmalade into hot sterilised jars; seal while hot.

MAKES ABOUT 1.75 LITRES

thick-cut orange, ginger & grapefruit marmalade

2 MEDIUM GRAPEFRUIT (850g)
2 MEDIUM ORANGES (480g)
1.75 LITRES WATER
1.5kg SUGAR, APPROXIMATELY
2 TABLESPOONS GRATED FRESH GINGER

1   Cut fruit in half, remove and discard seeds. Cut fruit into quarters, then cut quarters into thick slices. Combine fruit with the water in large bowl; cover, refrigerate overnight.
2   Transfer fruit mixture to large saucepan; bring to a boil. Reduce heat; simmer, covered, about 45 minutes or until fruit is soft.
3   Measure fruit mixture, allow 1 cup sugar to each cup of fruit mixture. Return fruit mixture with sugar and ginger to pan; stir over heat, without boiling, until sugar dissolves. Boil, uncovered, stirring occasionally, about 40 minutes or until marmalade jells when tested.
4   Pour hot marmalade into hot sterilised jars; seal while hot.

MAKES ABOUT 1.75 LITRES

three fruit marmalade

4 LARGE ORANGES (880g)
2 MEDIUM LEMONS (360g)
1 MEDIUM GRAPEFRUIT (390g)
1.25 LITRES WATER
1.5kg SUGAR, APPROXIMATELY

1   Cut unpeeled fruit in half, cut halves into thin slices. Remove seeds, tie in piece of muslin. Combine fruit, muslin bag and water in bowl, cover; stand overnight.
2   Transfer mixture to large saucepan, bring to boil, simmer, covered for 1 hour or until rind is soft; discard bag.
3   Measure fruit mixture return to pan, add ¾ cup sugar to each cup of fruit mixture. Stir over heat, without boiling, until sugar is dissolved. Bring to boil, boil, uncovered, without stirring, for 40 minutes or until marmalade jells when tested.
4   Pour hot marmalade into hot sterilised jars; seal while hot.

MAKES ABOUT 1.75 LITRES

grapefruit & brandy

3 LARGE GRAPEFRUIT (1.5kg)
1 LITRE WATER
1.3kg SUGAR
80ml BRANDY

1 Coarsely chop unpeeled grapefruit, seeds and all; process until mixture is chopped finely. Combine grapefruit mixture and the water in large pan; bring to a boil. Reduce heat; simmer, covered, 30 minutes. Transfer mixture to large bowl, cover; stand overnight.
2 Return fruit mixture to pan with sugar; stir over heat, without boiling, until sugar dissolves. Boil, uncovered, stirring occasionally, about 20 minutes or until marmalade jells when tested. Stir in brandy, stand 5 minutes.
3 Pour hot marmalade into hot sterilised jars; seal while hot.

MAKES ABOUT 2 LITRES

grapefruit & ginger

2 MEDIUM LEMONS (360g)
2 MEDIUM GRAPEFRUIT (780g)
6cm PIECE FRESH GINGER, PEELED
2.5 LITRES WATER
1 TEASPOON TARTARIC ACID
2kg SUGAR
165g FINELY CHOPPED STEM GINGER

1 Peel lemons, chop rind roughly, chop flesh roughly, reserve seeds and juice. Peel grapefruit, chop rind into fine strips, reserve. Chop grapefruit flesh roughly, reserve seeds and juice.
2 Combine lemon and grapefruit flesh with reserved juice in large saucepan. Tie reserved seeds, lemon rind and fresh ginger in a piece of muslin, add to pan. Add grapefruit rind with water and tartaric acid.
3 Bring to boil, boil, uncovered, for 1½ hours or until rind is soft and mixture has reduced by half. Discard bag. Add sugar, stir over heat without boiling until sugar is dissolved, stir in stem ginger.
4 Bring to boil, boil, uncovered, without stirring, for 15 minutes or until marmalade jells when tested.
5 Pour hot marmalade into hot sterilised jars; seal while hot.

MAKES ABOUT 2 LITRES

chunky breakfast marmalade

4 LARGE SEVILLE ORANGES (800g)
2 MEDIUM LEMONS (360g)
1.5 LITRES WATER
1.5kg SUGAR

1 Cut unpeeled fruit into quarters, reserve centre pith. Cut each quarter into thick slices, reserve seeds. Tie reserved seeds and reserved pith in a piece of muslin. Combine fruit, muslin bag and water in large bowl, cover, stand overnight.
2 Transfer mixture to large saucepan, bring to boil, simmer, covered for 1½ hours or until rind is soft; discard bag.
3 Add sugar, stir over heat, without boiling, until sugar is dissolved. Bring to boil, boil, uncovered, without stirring, for 10 minutes or until marmalade jells when tested.
4 Pour hot marmalade into hot sterilised jars; seal while hot.

MAKES ABOUT 2 LITRES

orange apricot marmalade

3 LARGE ORANGES (750g)
125g DRIED APRICOTS, CHOPPED
2 LITRES WATER
2kg SUGAR, APPROXIMATELY

1 Cut unpeeled oranges in quarters, then into thin slices. Combine oranges, apricots and water in bowl, cover; stand overnight.
2 Transfer mixture to large saucepan, bring to boil, simmer, covered for 45 minutes or until rind is soft.
3 Measure fruit mixture, allow 1 cup sugar to each cup of fruit mixture. Add sugar, stir over heat, without boiling, until sugar is dissolved. Bring to boil, boil, uncovered, without stirring, for 40 minutes or until marmalade jells when tested.
4 Pour hot marmalade into hot sterilised jars; seal while hot.

MAKES ABOUT 2 LITRES

five fruit marmalade

1 MEDIUM GRAPEFRUIT (390g)
7 MEDIUM MANDARINS (735g)
1 SMALL LEMON (130g)
2 LARGE APPLES (400g)
2 MEDIUM PEARS (300g)
3 LITRES WATER
2.5kg SUGAR, APPROXIMATELY

1 Cut unpeeled fruit in half, cut halves into thin slices. Remove seeds, tie in piece of muslin. Combine fruit, muslin bag and water in bowl, cover; stand overnight
2 Transfer mixture to large saucepan, bring to boil, simmer, covered, for 1 hour or until rind is soft; discard bag.
3 Measure fruit mixture, allow ¾ cup sugar to each cup of fruit mixture. Return fruit mixture and sugar to pan stir over heat, without boiling, until sugar is dissolved. Bring to boil, boil, uncovered, without stirring, for 40 minutes or until marmalade jells when tested.
4 Pour hot marmalade into hot sterilised jars; seal while hot.

MAKES ABOUT 2.5 LITRES

TIP Always buy unwaxed lemons for jam and marmalade making. If you can't buy unwaxed, then a good scrub with a vegetable brush will remove most traces of wax.

tangy lemon marmalade

6 MEDIUM LEMONS (1kg)
1.75 LITRES WATER
1kg SUGAR

1 Cut rind thinly from lemons; slice finely. Cut pith from lemons; chop roughly, reserve. Cut flesh into thin slices; reserve seeds. Combine flesh and rind in large bowl with water. Tie reserved pith and seeds in piece of muslin; add to bowl, cover, stand overnight.
2 Transfer mixture to large saucepan, bring to boil, simmer, covered, for 40 minutes or until rind is soft; discard muslin bag. Add sugar, stir over heat, without boiling, until sugar dissolves.
3 Bring to boil and boil, uncovered, without stirring, for 30 minutes or until marmalade jells when tested.
4 Pour hot marmalade into hot sterilised jars; seal while hot.

MAKES ABOUT 1.5 LITRES

pineapple & citrus fruit marmalade

2 MEDIUM GRAPEFRUIT (850g)
2 MEDIUM LIMES (160g)
2 MEDIUM ORANGES (480g)
1 LITRE WATER
1 SMALL PINEAPPLE (800g), PEELED, CHOPPED FINELY
1.3kg SUGAR, APPROXIMATELY
2 TABLESPOONS FRESH LIME JUICE

1 Peel rind thinly from grapefruit, limes and oranges, avoiding white pith. Cut rind into thin strips. Remove and discard pith from citrus fruit; reserve seeds, tie in piece of muslin. Chop citrus flesh finely. Combine rind, muslin bag, citrus flesh and the water in large bowl; cover, stand overnight.
2 Transfer fruit mixture to large saucepan, add pineapple; bring to a boil. Reduce heat; simmer, covered, about 45 minutes or until rind is very tender. Discard muslin bag.
3 Measure fruit mixture, allow 1 cup sugar to each cup of fruit mixture. Return fruit mixture with sugar to pan; stir over heat, without boiling, until sugar dissolves. Add juice; boil, uncovered, stirring occasionally, about 35 minutes or until marmalade jells when tested. Stand 5 minutes.
4 Pour hot marmalade into hot sterilised jars; seal while hot.

MAKES ABOUT 1.25 LITRES

TIP Fresh ginger is the thick gnarled root of a tropical plant. It can be kept, peeled, covered with dry sherry in a jar in the refrigerator, or can be frozen in an airtight container.

lime ginger marmalade

6 LARGE LIMES (600g)
1.5 LITRES WATER
1.5kg SUGAR, APPROXIMATELY
2 TEASPOONS GRATED FRESH GINGER

1   Slice unpeeled limes thinly, remove and discard seeds. Combine limes in large bowl with the water; cover, stand overnight.
2   Transfer lime mixture to large saucepan; bring to a boil. Reduce heat; simmer, covered, about 1 hour or until rind is tender.
3   Measure fruit mixture, allow 1 cup sugar to each cup of fruit mixture. Return fruit mixture with sugar to pan; stir over heat, without boiling, until sugar dissolves. Boil, uncovered, stirring occasionally, about 15 minutes or until marmalade jells when tested. Stir in ginger.
4   Pour hot marmalade into hot sterilised jars; seal while hot.

MAKES ABOUT 2 LITRES

lemon & lime marmalade

3 MEDIUM LEMONS (540g)
5 MEDIUM LIMES (425g)
2 LITRES WATER
1.75kg SUGAR, APPROXIMATELY
2 TABLESPOONS COINTREAU

1   Remove rind from fruit, cut into thin strips. Remove and reserve pith, chop flesh roughly, reserve seeds. Combine rind, flesh and water in large saucepan. Tie pith and seeds in a piece of muslin, add to pan.
2   Bring to boil, simmer, covered for 1 hour or until rind is soft; discard muslin bag.
3   Measure fruit mixture, add ¾ cup sugar to each cup of fruit mixture. Return fruit mixture with sugar to pan; stir over heat, without boiling, until sugar dissolves. Boil, uncovered, without stirring, for 20 minutes or until marmalade jells when tested. Stir in liqueur.
4   Pour hot marmalade into hot sterilised jars; seal while hot.

MAKES ABOUT 1.75 LITRES

lime & fig marmalade

10 LARGE LIMES (1kg)
2 LITRES WATER
1.3kg SUGAR, APPROXIMATELY
240g DRIED FIGS, SLICED THINLY

1 Remove rind from limes, cut rind into thin strips. Remove and reserve pith from limes; chop lime flesh coarsely, reserve seeds. Tie pith and seeds in piece of muslin. Combine rind, lime flesh, muslin bag and the water in large saucepan; bring to a boil. Reduce heat; simmer, covered, about 1 hour or until rind is soft. Discard muslin bag.
2 Measure fruit mixture, allow ¾ cup sugar to each cup of fruit mixture. Return fruit mixture with sugar to pan; stir over heat, without boiling, until sugar dissolves. Boil, uncovered, stirring occasionally, about 35 minutes or until marmalade jells when tested. Stir in figs.
3 Pour hot marmalade into hot sterilised jars; seal while hot.

MAKES ABOUT 1.75 LITRES

lemon coconut marmalade

8 MEDIUM LEMONS (1.1kg)
2 LITRES WATER
1.8kg SUGAR, APPROXIMATELY
50g FLAKED COCONUT, TOASTED

1 Cut unpeeled lemons in half lengthways; cut into thin slices, reserve seeds. Tie reserved lemon seeds in piece of muslin. Combine lemon slices, the water and muslin bag in large bowl; cover, stand overnight.
2 Transfer fruit mixture to large pan; bring to a boil. Reduce heat; simmer, covered, about 30 minutes or until rind is soft. Discard bag.
3 Measure fruit mixture, allow 1 cup sugar to each cup of fruit mixture. Return fruit mixture with sugar to pan; stir over heat, without boiling, until sugar dissolves. Boil, uncovered, stirring occasionally, about 45 minutes or until marmalade jells when tested. Stir in coconut.
4 Pour hot marmalade into hot sterilised jars; seal while hot.

MAKES ABOUT 2 LITRES

lemon & pineapple

2 MEDIUM PINEAPPLE (2kg), PEELED
2kg SUGAR
4 MEDIUM LEMONS (720g)
2 LITRES WATER

1 Halve pineapples, remove and reserve cores, slice flesh finely. Place flesh in large bowl, sprinkle with 440g sugar; cover, stand overnight. Slice unpeeled lemons finely, reserve seeds. Tie reserved seeds and chopped pineapple cores in piece of muslin. Combine lemon, muslin bag and water in large saucepan, bring to boil, simmer, uncovered, for 40 minutes or until rind is soft; discard muslin bag.
2 Stir in pineapple mixture and remaining sugar, stir over heat, without boiling, until sugar is dissolved. Bring to boil, boil, uncovered, without stirring ,for 20 minutes or until marmalade jells when tested.
3 Pour hot marmalade into hot sterilised jars; seal while hot.

MAKES ABOUT 2 LITRES

left: lime & fig marmalade; right: lemon coconut marmalade

TIP You will need about six passionfruit for this recipe.

marmalades

orange & passionfruit jelly marmalade

8 MEDIUM ORANGES (1.9kg)
125ml WATER
4 MEDIUM LEMONS (560g)
3 LITRES WATER, EXTRA
1.4kg SUGAR, APPROXIMATELY
125ml PASSIONFRUIT PULP

1 Using a zester, remove rind from two of the oranges, cover rind with the water; cover, stand 3 hours.
2 Meanwhile, coarsely chop the two zested oranges, remaining oranges and lemons. Combine fruits, including seeds and rind (but excluding the soaking orange rind), in large saucepan with the extra water; bring to a boil. Reduce heat; simmer, covered, about 1 hour or until rind is soft. Strain mixture through large piece of damp muslin into large bowl; allow mixture to drip through cloth for several hours or overnight. Do not squeeze or press the mixture through the cloth as this will result in cloudy jelly.
3 Measure the strained liquid, discard pulp. Allow ¾ cup sugar to each cup of liquid. Return liquid with sugar and drained orange rind to clean large saucepan; stir over heat, without boiling, until sugar dissolves. Boil, uncovered, without stirring, about 45 minutes or until marmalade jells when tested. Stir in passionfruit pulp; stand 5 minutes.
4 Pour hot marmalade into hot sterilised jars; seal while hot.

MAKES ABOUT 1.75 LITRES

apricot lemon marmalade

I LARGE ORANGE (300g)
2 LARGE LEMONS (360g)
2 TABLESPOONS WATER
250g DRIED APRICOTS
1.75 LITRES WATER, EXTRA
2kg SUGAR, APPROXI-
MATELY

1 Remove and reserve seeds from unpeeled quartered orange and lemons. Put seeds and the 2 tablespoons of water in small bowl, cover; set aside. Blend or process chopped orange, lemons and apricots, in batches, until finely chopped.

2 Combine fruit mixture with the extra water in large saucepan; bring to a boil. Reduce heat; simmer, covered, 45 minutes. Transfer mixture to large heatproof bowl, cover. Stand fruit mixture and seed mixture, separately, overnight.

3 Drain seeds over small bowl; reserve liquid, discard seeds. Measure fruit mixture; allow I cup sugar to each cup of fruit mixture. Return fruit mixture with reserved seed liquid to pan; bring to a boil. Add sugar; stir over heat, without boiling, until sugar dissolves. Boil, uncovered, stirring occasionally, about 30 minutes or until marmalade jells when tested. Stand 5 minutes.

4 Pour hot marmalade into hot sterilised jars; seal while hot.

MAKES ABOUT 2 LITRES

chutneys & relishes

tomato & apple chutney

2kg RIPE TOMATOES, PEELED, CHOPPED
400g APPLES
240g ONIONS, CHOPPED
330g RAW SUGAR

1.25 LITRES MALT VINEGAR
2 TEASPOONS GROUND GINGER
½ TEASPOON GROUND CINNAMON
½ TEASPOON GROUND CLOVES

1 Combine all ingredients in large saucepan.
2 Stir over heat, without boiling, until sugar is dissolved.
3 Bring to boil; simmer, uncovered, stirring occasionally, for 1½ hours or until mixture is thick.
4 Spoon hot chutney into hot sterilised jars; seal while hot.

MAKES ABOUT 1.75 LITRES

A condiment of Indian origin, chutney is a type of tangy sweet pickle served as an accompaniment to curries, hot and cold meats and savouries. There are many varieties, all based on chopped fruit and/or vegetables, sugar and vinegar. Not much can go wrong as mixtures are simply cooked until thick. Once you have opened a jar, keep, covered, in the fridge. For best results, be sure to read our tips for success on pages 4–9 before you start.

spicy tomato chutney

1kg RIPE TOMATOES, PEELED, CHOPPED
400g APPLES, PEELED, CHOPPED
240g ONIONS, CHOPPED
375ml MALT VINEGAR
220g BROWN SUGAR,
¼ TEASPOON CHILLI POWDER

½ TEASPOON MUSTARD POWDER
120g SULTANAS
1 CLOVE GARLIC CRUSHED
2 TEASPOONS CURRY POWDER
2 TEASPOON GROUND ALLSPICE

1 Combine all ingredients in large saucepan.
2 Stir over heat, without boiling, until sugar is dissolved.
3 Bring to boil; simmer, uncovered, stirring occasionally, for 1 hour or until mixture is thick.
4 Spoon hot chutney into hot sterilised jars; seal while hot.

MAKES ABOUT 1.5 LITRES

sweet fruit chutney

1kg APPLES, PEELED, CHOPPED
1kg TOMATOES, PEELED, CHOPPED
500kg ONIONS, CHOPPED
240g SULTANAS
120g CHOPPED RAISINS
150g CURRANTS
1 LITRE MALT VINEGAR
1kg BROWN SUGAR
2 TEASPOONS GRATED ORANGE RIND
2 TEASPOONS GRATED FRESH GINGER
½ TEASPOON GROUND CLOVES
2 TEASPOONS GROUND CINNAMON
PINCH CAYENNE PEPPER

1 Combine all ingredients in large saucepan.
2 Stir over heat, without boiling, until sugar is dissolved. Bring to boil; simmer, uncovered, stirring occasionally, for 1½ hours, or until mixture is thick.
3 Spoon hot chutney into hot sterilised jars; seal while hot.

MAKES ABOUT 1.5 LITRES

tomato chutney

8 MEDIUM TOMATOES (1.5kg)
3 MEDIUM WHITE ONIONS (450g), CHOPPED FINELY
300g BROWN SUGAR
375ml MALT VINEGAR
1½ TABLESPOONS MUSTARD POWDER
1 TABLESPOON MILD CURRY POWDER
½ TEASPOON CAYENNE PEPPER
2 TEASPOONS COARSE COOKING SALT

1 Peel and coarsely chop tomatoes; combine with remaining ingredients in large heavy-base saucepan. Stir over heat, without boiling, until sugar dissolves.
2 Simmer, uncovered, stirring occasionally, about 1¼ hours or until mixture thickens.
3 Spoon hot chutney into hot sterilised jars; seal while hot.

MAKES ABOUT 1 LITRE

TIP Brown malt vinegar is made from fermented malt and beech shavings and is very familiar to many fans of fish and chips!

TIP The walnuts used here are the more common large variety, not the small black ones used for pickling.

pear & walnut chutney

9 SMALL PEARS (1.6kg), PEELED, CHOPPED COARSELY

2 LARGE APPLES (400g), PEELED, CHOPPED COARSELY

250ml WHITE VINEGAR

180ml LEMON JUICE

200g BROWN SUGAR

170g COARSELY CHOPPED RAISINS

160g COARSELY CHOPPED PITTED DATES

120g COARSELY CHOPPED WALNUTS

1 Combine ingredients in large heavy-based saucepan; bring to a boil.

2 Simmer, uncovered, stirring occasionally, about 1¼ hours or until mixture thickens.

3 Spoon hot chutney into hot sterilised jars; seal while hot.

MAKES ABOUT 1.25 LITRES

dried fruit chutney

200g CHOPPED DRIED PEARS

200g CHOPPED DRIED APRICOTS

200g CHOPPED DATES

200g CHOPPED DRIED APPLES

200g SULTANAS

1 LITRE WATER

500ml CIDER VINEGAR

440g BROWN SUGAR

½ TEASPOON CHILLI POWDER

½ TEASPOON TURMERIC

½ TEASPOON GROUND NUTMEG

½ TEASPOON GROUND GINGER

1 CLOVE GARLIC, CRUSHED

1 Combine pears, apricots, dates, apples, sultanas and water in a large bowl, cover and stand overnight.

2 Combine undrained fruit mixture, with remaining ingredients in large saucepan. Stir over heat, without boiling, until sugar is dissolved. Bring to boil simmer, uncovered, stirring occasionally, for 1¼ hours or until mixture is thick.

3 Spoon hot chutney into hot sterilised jars; seal while hot.

MAKES ABOUT 1.75 LITRES

apple & grape chutney

800g APPLES, PEELED, CHOPPED
1kg SEEDLESS WHITE GRAPES
HALVED
170g RAISINS
250ml CIDER VINEGAR
½ TEASPOON GRATED LEMON RIND
125ml LEMON JUICE
½ TEASPOON GROUND ALLSPICE
½ TEASPOON GROUND CLOVES
½ TEASPOON GROUND GINGER
¼ TEASPOON GROUND
CINNAMON
½ TEASPOON SALT
¼ TEASPOON PAPRIKA
660g BROWN SUGAR

1 Combine apples, grapes, raisins, vinegar, rind, lemon juice, spices, salt and paprika in large saucepan. Bring to boil simmer, uncovered, stirring occasionally, for 1 hour or until fruit is soft.
2 Add sugar, stir over heat, without boiling, until sugar is dissolved.
3 Bring to boil, simmer, uncovered, stirring occasionally, for 30 minutes or until thick.
4 Spoon hot chutney into hot sterilised jars; seal while hot.

MAKES ABOUT 1.75 LITRES

apple & red pepper chutney

2 TEASPOONS BLACK PEPPERCORNS
1 TEASPOON CLOVES
2 LARGE APPLES (400g), PEELED, CHOPPED FINELY
3 MEDIUM RED PEPPERS (600g), CHOPPED FINELY
2 MEDIUM WHITE ONIONS (300g), CHOPPED FINELY
2 CLOVES GARLIC, CRUSHED
75g CURRANTS
500ml CIDER VINEGAR
125ml DRY WHITE WINE
625ml WATER
300g BROWN SUGAR

1 Tie peppercorns and cloves in piece of muslin. Place muslin bag in large heavy-based saucepan with apple, peppers, onion, garlic, currants, vinegar, wine and the water; bring to a boil. Simmer, uncovered, stirring occasionally, about 15 minutes or until apple and pepper are soft.
2 Add sugar; stir over heat, without boiling, until sugar dissolves. Simmer, uncovered, stirring occasionally, about 1½ hours or until mixture thickens. Discard bag.
3 Spoon hot chutney into hot sterilised jars; seal while hot.

MAKES ABOUT 750ml

minted apple & apricot chutney

300g DRIED APRICOTS, CHOPPED
800g APPLES, PEELED, CHOPPED
250ml WHITE VINEGAR
240g ONIONS, CHOPPED
550g BROWN SUGAR
3 TABLESPOONS CHOPPED
FRESH MINT
120g SULTANAS

1 Place apricots in bowl, cover with cold water, stand overnight. Drain apricots.
2 Combine apricots with remaining ingredients in large saucepan, stir over heat, without boiling, until sugar is dissolved.
3 Bring to boil, simmer, uncovered, stirring occasionally, for about 45 minutes or until mixture is thick.
4 Spoon hot chutney into hot sterilised jars; seal while hot.

MAKES ABOUT 1.5 LITRES

green mango chutney

6 GREEN MANGOES (2kg), PEELED, CHOPPED COARSELY
1 TABLESPOON COARSE COOKING SALT
385g WHITE SUGAR
625ml MALT VINEGAR
8cm PIECE GINGER (40G), GRATED
2 CLOVES GARLIC, CRUSHED
110g COARSELY CHOPPED DATES
120g CHOPPED RAISINS
1 TEASPOON CHILLI POWDER
1 TEASPOON GROUND CINNAMON
1 TEASPOON GROUND CUMIN

1 Place mangoes and salt in large bowl. Barely cover with cold water, cover; stand overnight. Drain mangoes; discard water.
2 Stir sugar and vinegar in large saucepan over heat, without boiling, until sugar dissolves. Stir in mangoes and remaining ingredients; bring to boil, simmer, uncovered, stirring occasionally, for 45 minutes or until mixture is thick.
3 Spoon hot chutney into hot sterilised jars; seal while hot.

MAKES ABOUT 2 LITRES

chutneys & relishes

TIP Green, or unripe, mangoes have firm flesh, that is better suited to chutney-making than the ripe variety.

apricot chutney

1kg APRICOTS, CHOPPED
360g ONIONS, CHOPPED
160g SULTANAS
220g BROWN SUGAR
2 TEASPOONS GRATED FRESH GINGER
1 SMALL FRESH GREEN CHILLI, CHOPPED
500ml MALT VINEGAR
125ml BRANDY

1   Combine apricots, onions, sultanas, sugar, ginger, chilli and vinegar in large saucepan. Stir over heat, without boiling, until sugar is dissolved.
2   Bring to boil, simmer, uncovered, stirring occasionally, for 1½ hours or until mixture is thick. Stir in brandy.
3   Pour into hot sterilised jars; seal while hot.

MAKES ABOUT 1.25 LITRES

apricot & apple chutney

500g APRICOTS, PITTED, CHOPPED
400g APPLES, PEELED, CHOPPED
240g ONIONS, CHOPPED
375ml WHITE VINEGAR
85g CHOPPED DATES
2 TEASPOONS GRATED FRESH GINGER
330g BROWN SUGAR
1 TABLESPOON MUSTARD POWDER
2 CLOVES GARLIC, CRUSHED
1 TEASPOON BLACK MUSTARD SEEDS
½ TEASPOON GROUND CUMIN
¼ TEASPOON GROUND CARDAMOM
½ TEASPOON GROUND CORIANDER

1   Combine all ingredients in large saucepan, stir over heat, without boiling, until sugar is dissolved.
2   Bring to boil, simmer, uncovered, stirring occasionally, for 1 hour or until mixture is thick.
3   Pour into hot sterilised jars.; seal while hot.

MAKES ABOUT 1.25 LITRES

peach & cardamom chutney

7 LARGE PEACHES (1.5kg)
1 LARGE ONION (200g), CHOPPED FINELY
120g COARSELY CHOPPED RAISINS
330g BROWN SUGAR
180ml CIDER VINEGAR
1 CINNAMON STICK
4 CARDAMOM PODS, BRUISED
1 TEASPOON WHOLE ALLSPICE
2 TEASPOONS FINELY GRATED LEMON RIND

1   Cut small cross in bottom of each peach. Lower gently into large saucepan of boiling water, boil for 1 minute, then place in large bowl of cold water. Peel peaches, remove stones, chop peaches coarsely.
2   Combine peaches with remaining ingredients in large saucepan; stir over heat until sugar dissolves. Bring to the boil; reduce heat. Simmer, uncovered, stirring occasionally, about 45 minutes or until thick.
3   Pour chutney into hot sterilised jars; seal while hot.

MAKES ABOUT 2 LITRES

right: peach & cardamom chutney

TIP Aubergines need to be sliced and salted to reduce their bitterness. Rinse and dry well before use.

aubergine chutney

1 MEDIUM AUBERGINE (300g), PEELED, CHOPPED COARSELY

70g COARSE COOKING SALT

1 MEDIUM ONION (150g), CHOPPED COARSELY

2 MEDIUM TOMATOES (300g), DESEEDED, CHOPPED COARSELY

1 SMALL GREEN PEPPER (150g), CHOPPED COARSELY

2 CLOVES GARLIC, CRUSHED

125ml CIDER VINEGAR

125ml WHITE VINEGAR

1 TEASPOON CHILLI POWDER

1 TEASPOON GROUND TURMERIC

110g BROWN SUGAR

1 Place aubergine in colander; sprinkle with salt; stand 30 minutes. Rinse aubergine, pat dry.

2 Combine aubergine, onion, tomato, pepper, garlic, vinegars, chilli and turmeric in large saucepan; simmer, uncovered, stirring occasionally, about 45 minutes or until vegetables are pulpy.

3 Stir in sugar; cook, stirring, over low heat, until sugar dissolves.

4 Spoon hot chutney into hot sterilised jars; seal while hot.

MAKES ABOUT 750ml

banana chutney

7 MEDIUM (1kg) BANANAS, CHOPPED

500g DATES, CHOPPED

1 TEASPOON GRATED FRESH GINGER

1 MEDIUM (120g) ONION, CHOPPED

500ml MALT VINEGAR

2 TEASPOONS GRATED LEMON RIND

60ml LEMON JUICE

220g BROWN SUGAR

2 TEASPOONS CURRY POWDER

1 Combine bananas, dates, ginger, onion, vinegar, rind and lemon juice, in large saucepan. Bring to boil simmer, uncovered, for 20 minutes or until fruit is soft.

2 Add sugar and curry powder, stir over heat, without boiling, until sugar is dissolved. Bring to boil, simmer, uncovered, stirring occasionally, for 20 minutes or until mixture is thick.

3 Spoon hot chutney into hot sterilised jars; seal while hot.

MAKES ABOUT 1.25 LITRES

fig, tomato & caramelised onion jam

I TABLESPOON OLIVE OIL
4 MEDIUM ONIONS (600g), SLICED THINLY
2 TABLESPOONS WHITE WINE VINEGAR
55g SUGAR
6 LARGE TOMATOES (1.5kg), PEELED, CHOPPED
700g DRIED FIGS, SLICED
125ml LEMON JUICE
880g SUGAR, EXTRA

1 Heat oil in large frying pan, add onion; cook, stirring, about 15 minutes or until onion is very soft. Add vinegar and sugar; cook, stirring often, about 20 minutes or until mixture is lightly browned.
2 Meanwhile, combine tomato and figs in large heavy-based pan. Simmer, uncovered, about 20 minutes or until fruit is pulpy. Add onion mixture and remaining ingredients; stir over heat, without boiling, until extra sugar is dissolved. Boil, uncovered, stirring occasionally, about 20 minutes or until jam jells when tested on a cold saucer.
3 Pour hot jam into hot sterilised jars; seal while hot.

MAKES ABOUT 1.5 LITRES

rhubarb & tomato chutney

I TABLESPOON OLIVE OIL
1½ TABLESPOONS BLACK MUSTARD SEEDS
1½ TABLESPOONS GROUND CUMIN
½ TEASPOON GROUND CLOVES
1½ TABLESPOONS GROUND CORIANDER
11 MEDIUM TOMATOES (2kg), CHOPPED COARSELY
2 LARGE WHITE ONIONS (400g), CHOPPED FINELY
I TEASPOON COARSE COOKING SALT
2 CLOVES GARLIC, CRUSHED
340g RAISINS
200g BROWN SUGAR
250ml MALT VINEGAR
700g CHOPPED FRESH RHUBARB STEMS

1 Heat oil in large heavy-based saucepan; cook seeds and spices, stirring, until fragrant. Add tomatoes, onion, salt, garlic, raisins, sugar and vinegar. Stir over heat, without boiling, until sugar dissolves.
2 Simmer, uncovered, stirring occasionally, about 35 minutes or until mixture thickens. Stir in rhubarb; simmer, uncovered, stirring occasionally, about 5 minutes or until rhubarb is tender.
3 Spoon hot chutney into hot sterilised jars; seal while hot.

MAKES ABOUT 2 LITRES

left: rhubarb & tomato chutney; right: fig, tomato & caramelised onion jam

blackberry relish

1kg BLACKBERRIES
125ml WATER
1 TABLESPOON SUGAR
1 TEASPOON MUSTARD POWDER
1 TEASPOON GROUND ALLSPICE
½ TEASPOON GROUND
CINNAMON
250ml MALT VINEGAR

1   Combine half the blackberries and the water in large saucepan. Bring to boil, simmer, covered, for 10 minutes or until berries are soft. Blend or process mixture until smooth, return to pan. Stir in remaining ingredients.
2   Bring to boil, simmer, uncovered, stirring occasionally, for around 15 minutes or until mixture is thick.
3   Pour hot relish into hot sterilised jars; seal while hot.

MAKES ABOUT 1 LITRE

apricot relish

1kg APRICOTS
240g ONIONS, FINELY CHOPPED
1 TABLESPOON GRATED FRESH
GINGER
80g SULTANAS
220g SUGAR
2 TEASPOONS FRENCH MUSTARD
½ TEASPOON GROUND CINNAMON
500ml CIDER VINEGAR

1   Halve apricots, discard stones. Combine with remaining ingredients in large pan. Stir over heat, without boiling, until sugar dissolves.
2   Bring to boil, simmer, uncovered, stirring occasionally, for 1½ hours or until mixture is thick.
3   Pour hot relish into hot sterilised jars; seal while hot.

MAKES ABOUT 1 LITRE

tomato kasaundi

4 LARGE TOMATOES (880g), CHOPPED COARSELY
1 MEDIUM ONION (150g), CHOPPED COARSELY
4 CLOVES GARLIC, CHOPPED COARSELY
3cm PIECE FRESH GINGER (15g), CHOPPED FINELY
4 FRESH SMALL RED THAI CHILLIES, CHOPPED COARSELY
2 TEASPOONS GROUND CUMIN
½ TEASPOON GROUND TURMERIC
½ TEASPOON CHILLI POWDER
¼ TEASPOON GROUND CLOVES
2 TABLESPOONS VEGETABLE OIL
60ml WHITE VINEGAR
75g MALT SUGAR

1   Blend or process ingredients until smooth. Transfer mixture to large saucepan; cook, stirring, without boiling, until sugar is dissolved.
2   Simmer, uncovered, stirring occasionally, about 45 minutes or until kasaundi thickens slightly.
3   Pour hot relish into hot sterilised jars; seal while hot.

MAKES ABOUT 750ml

right: tomato kasaundi

■ Sharp, tangy relishes are based on fruit and/ or vegetables and usually contain vinegar and sugar but generally not in large enough quantities to preserve the ingredients for as long as most other pickles. Relishes must be kept in the fridge and will keep for about a month. They add zest to hot or cold meats, curries and savoury snacks. Be sure to read our hints for success on bottling before you start.

green tomato & pear chutney

4 SMALL UNDER-RIPE PEARS (720g), PEELED, CHOPPED
7 MEDIUM UNDER-RIPE TOMATOES (1.3kg), CHOPPED
2 LARGE ONIONS (400g), CHOPPED
150g CURRANTS
45g BLACK MUSTARD SEEDS
500ml MALT VINEGAR
400g BROWN SUGAR
2 TEASPOONS SALT
1 TABLESPOON GROUND CORIANDER
1 TABLESPOON GROUND GINGER
2 TEASPOONS GROUND CARDAMOM

1   Combine ingredients in large saucepan, stir over heat, without boiling, until sugar is dissolved. Simmer, uncovered, stirring occasionally, about 1 hour or until thick.
2   Spoon hot chutney into hot sterilised jars; seal while hot.

MAKES ABOUT 1.75 LITRES

TIP Balsamic vinegar is made from an Italian regional wine of white trebbiano grapes specially processed then aged in antique wooden casks to give an exquisite pungent flavour.

tomato, aubergine & pepper relish

2 SMALL AUBERGINES (460g)
1 TABLESPOON COARSE COOKING SALT
3 MEDIUM RED PEPPERS (600g)
2 TABLESPOONS OLIVE OIL
1 LARGE WHITE ONION (200g), SLICED THINLY
1 CLOVE GARLIC, CRUSHED
2 TEASPOONS BLACK MUSTARD SEEDS
3 TEASPOONS CUMIN SEEDS
¼ TEASPOON CARDAMOM SEEDS
6 MEDIUM TOMATOES (1.1kg), PEELED, DESEEDED, CHOPPED COARSELY
180ml WHITE WINE VINEGAR
60ml RED WINE VINEGAR
1 TABLESPOON BALSAMIC VINEGAR
75g BROWN SUGAR

1   Cut aubergines into 2cm slices; place on wire rack, sprinkle with salt. Stand 10 minutes. Rinse slices under cold water; drain on absorbent paper. Chop aubergine slices coarsely.
2   Quarter peppers, remove and discard seeds and membranes. Roast under grill or in very hot oven, skin-side up, until skin blisters and blackens. Cover pepper pieces with cling film or paper for 5 minutes, peel away skin. Chop pepper coarsely.
3   Heat oil in large heavy-based saucepan; cook onion, garlic and seeds, stirring, until onion is soft. Add aubergine; cook, stirring, until aubergine is browned lightly. Add pepper and remaining ingredients; simmer, covered, stirring occasionally, 50 minutes. Remove lid; simmer about 10 minutes or until mixture thickens.
4   Spoon hot relish into hot sterilised jars; seal while hot.

MAKES ABOUT 1 LITRE

chutneys & relishes

left: corn relish;
right: spicy green tomato relish

spicy green tomato relish

5 MEDIUM GREEN TOMATOES (1kg), SLICED
1 MEDIUM ONION (150g), SLICED
1kg GHERKIN CUCUMBERS, CHOPPED
1 SMALL GREEN PEPPER (150g), CHOPPED
6 TABLESPOONS COARSE COOKING SALT
500ml CIDER VINEGAR
250ml WHITE VINEGAR
1 TEASPOON MUSTARD POWDER
½ TEASPOON GROUND ALLSPICE
¼ TEASPOON MIXED SPICE
¼ TEASPOON GROUND CINNAMON
¼ TEASPOON GROUND BLACK PEPPER
200g BROWN SUGAR

1 Combine vegetables in large bowl, sprinkle with salt, cover; stand several hours. Rinse under cold water; drain well.
2 Combine vegetables, vinegars and spices in large saucepan. Bring to a boil; simmer, uncovered, stirring occasionally, about 45 minutes or until vegetables are pulpy. Add sugar; stir over heat, without boiling, until sugar is dissolved. Bring to a boil; boil, uncovered, 15 minutes.
3 Pour into hot sterilised jars; seal while hot.

MAKES ABOUT 1.25 LITRES

corn relish

3 X 440g CANS CORN KERNELS, DRAINED
3 SMALL ONIONS (240g), CHOPPED
1 SMALL RED PEPPER (150g), CHOPPED
1 SMALL GREEN PEPPER (150g), CHOPPED
2 STICKS CELERY (150g), CHOPPED
500ml CIDER VINEGAR
430ml WHITE VINEGAR
220g SUGAR
1 TABLESPOON MUSTARD POWDER
1 TABLESPOON YELLOW MUSTARD SEEDS
1 TEASPOON GROUND TURMERIC
½ TEASPOON GROUND CLOVES
3 TABLESPOONS CORNFLOUR
60ml WHITE VINEGAR, EXTRA

1 Combine corn, onion, peppers, celery, vinegars, sugar, mustard, seeds, turmeric and cloves in large saucepan. Bring to a boil; simmer, uncovered, about 45 minutes, stirring occasionally, or until mixture thickens slightly. Stir in blended cornflour and extra vinegar; stir until mixture boils and thickens.
2 Pour into hot sterilised jars; seal while hot.

MAKES ABOUT 1.5 LITRES

chutneys & relishes

GREEN TOMATOES
Green tomatoes are **a** medium-sized variety with a piquant flavour which is well suited to chutneys and relishes.

courgette & apple relish

750g COURGETTES, GRATED
1½ TABLESPOON COARSE
COOKING SALT
600g APPLES, PEELED, CHOPPED
500g ONIONS, CHOPPED
250g RAISINS, CHOPPED
500ml MALT VINEGAR
165g BROWN SUGAR
½ TEASPOON GARAM MASALA
½ TEASPOON GROUND
CORIANDER

1 Place courgettes in colander, sprinkle with salt, stand 2 hours, rinse under cold water; drain on absorbent paper.
2 Combine courgettes, apples, onions, raisins and vinegar in large saucepan. Bring to boil, simmer, covered, for 20 minutes or until mixture is pulpy. Stir in sugar and spices, stir over heat until sugar is dissolved. Bring to boil, simmer, uncovered, stirring occasionally, for 20 minutes or until mixture is thick.
3 Spoon hot relish into hot sterilised jars; seal while hot.

MAKES ABOUT 1.5 LITRES

sweet & sour relish

1 MEDIUM PINEAPPLE (1.25kg),
PEELED, CHOPPED FINELY
2 TEASPOONS COARSE
COOKING SALT
1 LITRE MALT VINEGAR
1 TABLESPOON GRATED FRESH
GINGER
2 CLOVES GARLIC, CRUSHED
2 MEDIUM WHITE ONIONS (300g),
CHOPPED FINELY
1 SMALL RED PEPPER (150G),
CHOPPED FINELY
1 TABLESPOON TOMATO PASTE
500ml WATER
330g SUGAR

1 Place pineapple in large bowl, sprinkle with salt. Cover; stand overnight. Rinse pineapple under cold water; drain well.
2 Combine pineapple, vinegar, ginger, garlic, onion, pepper, paste and the water in large heavy-based saucepan; bring to a boil. Simmer, uncovered, 30 minutes. Add sugar; stir over heat, without boiling, until sugar dissolves. Simmer, uncovered, stirring occasionally, about 30 minutes or until mixture thickens.
3 Spoon hot relish into hot sterilised jars; seal while hot.

MAKES ABOUT 1 LITRE

TIP The dried, star-shaped seed pod star anise has a slight liquorice-like taste, but it should not be confused with anise, being far more spicily pungent, with overtones of clove and cinnamon.

250ml CIDER VINEGAR
110g RAW SUGAR
½ TEASPOON MILD CURRY POWDER
½ TEASPOON MUSTARD POWDER
2 CUCUMBERS (520g), PEELED, CHOPPED FINELY
4 SMALL TOMATOES (520g), CHOPPED FINELY
85g RAISINS
12 TABLESPOONS FINELY CHOPPED FRESH MINT LEAVES

mint relish

1 Combine vinegar, sugar, curry powder and mustard powder in large saucepan; stir over heat, without boiling, until sugar dissolves.
2 Bring to a boil. Remove pan from heat; stir in remaining ingredients.
3 Spoon hot relish into hot sterilised jars; seal while hot.

MAKES ABOUT 1 LITRE

oriental relish

1 MEDIUM LEMON (180g)
1 LARGE ORANGE (220g)
1 MEDIUM ONION (120g), GRATED
2 x 425g CANS TOMATOES
600g APPLES, PEELED, CHOPPED
1 CINNAMON STICK
2 STAR ANISE
2 TABLESPOONS GRATED FRESH GINGER
1 TEASPOON GROUND ALLSPICE
½ TEASPOON CARDAMOM SEEDS
330g BROWN SUGAR
180ml MALT VINEGAR
250ml WATER

1 Chop unpeeled lemon and orange; discard seeds. Blend or process lemon and orange until almost smooth.
2 Combine lemon mixture, onion, undrained crushed tomatoes and remaining ingredients in large saucepan. Stir over heat, without boiling, until sugar is dissolved. Bring to boil, simmer, uncovered, stirring occasionally, for 1½ hours or until mixture is thick. Discard cinnamon sticks and star anise.
3 Spoon hot relish into hot sterilised jars; seal while hot.

MAKES ABOUT 1.75 LITRES

pickles

spicy mustard pickles

¼ CAULIFLOWER (500g), CHOPPED
250g GREEN BEANS, CHOPPED
3 MEDIUM ONIONS (360g), CHOPPED
1 MEDIUM RED PEPPER (150g,) CHOPPED
60g COARSE COOKING SALT
2 TABLESPOONS WHOLEGRAIN
MUSTARD

2 TEASPOONS MUSTARD POWDER
3 TEASPOONS CURRY POWDER
¼ TEASPOON TURMERIC
430ml WHITE VINEGAR
220g BROWN SUGAR,
2 TABLESPOONS PLAIN FLOUR
60ml WHITE VINEGAR, EXTRA

1 Combine cauliflower, beans, onions and pepper in large bowl, sprinkle with salt, cover; stand overnight. Rinse vegetables under cold water; drain. Combine vegetables, mustards, curry powder, turmeric, vinegar and sugar in large pan.
2 Stir over heat, without boiling, until sugar is dissolved. Bring to boil, simmer, uncovered, for 10 minutes or until vegetables are just tender. Stir in blended flour and extra vinegar, stir over heat until mixture boils and thickens.
3 Pour into hot sterilised jars; seal when cold.

MAKES ABOUT 1 LITRE

Pickles mostly fall into two categories: those that have a clear, sweet and/or spicy vinegar poured over various vegetables, or those that are thick and pulpy. These are thickened either by slow cooking to evaporate the liquid and concentrate the flavours, or by thickening the liquid with flour. All pickles need to be refrigerated after opening. Before starting, read our tips & techniques on pages 4–9.

corn pickle

3 MEDIUM ONIONS (360g), CHOPPED
1 CUCUMBER (280g), CHOPPED
1 GREEN PEPPER (150g), CHOPPED
4 TOMATOES (400g), PEELED, CHOPPED
2 × 440g CANS CORN KERNELS,
DRAINED
625ml CIDER VINEGAR

125ml WATER
220g SUGAR
2 TEASPOONS COARSE COOKING SALT
2 TEASPONS MUSTARD POWDER
½ TEASPOON TURMERIC
35g CORNFLOUR
125ml WATER, EXTRA

1 Combine onions, cucumber, pepper, tomatoes, corn, vinegar, water, sugar, salt, mustard and turmeric in large pan. Bring to boil, simmer, covered, stirring occasionally, for 1 hour. Stir in blended cornflour and extra water, stir over heat until mixture boils and thickens.
2 Pour into hot sterilised jars; seal when cold.

MAKES ABOUT 2.5 LITRES

curried green tomatoes

1kg GREEN TOMATOES, SLICED
1 LARGE ONION (170g), SLICED
1 SMALL CUCUMBER (150g), SLICED
1 STICK CELERY, SLICED
60g COARSE COOKING SLAT
500ml WHITE VINEGAR
220g SUGAR
½ TEASPOON CAYENNE PEPPER
2 TEASPOONS CURRY POWDER
2 TEASPOONS MUSTARD POWDER
35g CORNFLOUR
125ml WHITE VINEGAR, EXTRA

1 Combine tomatoes, onion, cucumber and celery in large bowl, sprinkle with salt, cover; stand overnight.
2 Rinse vegetables under cold water; drain well. Combine vinegar and sugar in large saucepan. Stir over heat, without boiling, until sugar is dissolved.
3 Stir in vegetables, cayenne, curry powder, mustard and blended cornflour and extra vinegar. stir over heat until mixture boils and thickens.
4 Spoon into hot sterilised jars; seal when cold.

MAKES ABOUT 1.25 LITRES

spicy mixed pickles

250g CAULIFLOWER, CHOPPED
250g PICKLING ONIONS
240g CARROTS, SLICED
250g PEAS

SPICED VINEGAR
2 SMALL RED CHILLIES, CHOPPED
6 CLOVES
875ml WHITE VINEGAR
165g SUGAR

1 Bring large saucepan of water to boil, add vegetables, bring back to boil, drain; cool.
2 Pack vegetables into large sterilised jar, cover completely with spiced vinegar; seal.

SPICED VINEGAR Combine chillies, cloves, vinegar and sugar in saucepan. Stir over heat without boiling, until sugar is dissolved, cool, discard cloves.

cauliflower & pepper pickle

I SMALL CAULIFLOWER (700g), CHOPPED COARSELY
2 MEDIUM WHITE ONIONS (300g), CHOPPED COARSELY
I MEDIUM RED PEPPER (200g), CHOPPED COARSELY
I TABLESPOON COARSE COOKING SALT
250ml WHITE VINEGAR
110g SUGAR
½ TEASPOON GROUND ALLSPICE
2 CLOVES
I DRIED BAY LEAF
I TABLESPOON MILD CURRY POWDER
I TABLESPOON MUSTARD POWDER
I TABLESPOON WHOLEGRAIN MUSTARD
I TEASPOON GROUND TURMERIC
I TABLESPOON PLAIN FLOUR
60ml WHITE VINEGAR, EXTRA

1 Place cauliflower, onion and pepper in large bowl, sprinkle with salt. Cover; stand overnight.
2 Rinse vegetables under cold water; drain well. Combine vinegar, sugar, allspice, cloves and bay leaf in large saucepan; bring to a boil. Add vegetables; simmer, covered, about 20 minutes or until vegetables are just tender.
3 Stir in blended curry powder, mustards, turmeric, flour and extra vinegar; stir over heat until mixture boils and thickens. Spoon hot pickles into hot sterilised jars; seal while hot.

MAKES ABOUT I LITRE

sugar-free mixed pickles

½ CAULIFLOWER (1kg), CHOPPED
2 TEASPOONS COARSE COOKING SALT
I LARGE CUCUMBER (400g), CHOPPED
I GREEN PEPPER (150g), CHOPPED
I RED PEPPER (150g), CHOPPED

VINEGAR
500ml WHITE VINEGAR
2 TEASPOONS COARSE COOKING SALT
8 BLACK PEPPERCORNS
I BAY LEAF

1 Sprinkle cauliflower with I teaspoon of salt, cover; stand overnight.
2 Add cucumber and remaining salt, stand I hour. Rinse vegetables under cold water; drain.
3 Add vegetables to large saucepan of boiling water, boil 5 minutes or until just tender. Rinse vegetables under cold water, drain, cool.
4 Pack vegetables into large sterilised jar; cover completely with vinegar, seal.

VINEGAR Combine all ingredients in saucepan, bring to boil, simmer, uncovered 5 minutes; strain, cool.

Generally, you need large wide-mouthed jars for pickles preserved in vinegar, and the vegetables are chopped to suit your taste. In these cases, we haven't specified how much the recipe makes as it depends on the chopped size and how tightly the vegetables are packed into the jars. It is important that the ingredients are completely covered with the vinegar mixture to complete the pickling process and prevent the vegetables from deteriorating.

gherkins in spiced vinegar

1.5 LITRES WATER
180g COARSE COOKING SALT
2kg GHERKIN CUCUMBERS

SPICED VINEGAR
1 LITRE WHITE VINEGAR
495g SUGAR
2 CINNAMON STICKS
2 TEASPOONS BLACK PEPPERCORNS
2 TEASPOONS CLOVES

1   Combine water and salt in large saucepan, stir over heat until salt is dissolved; cool.
2   Wash gherkins well, place in large bowl, cover gherkins completely with salt water, cover; stand 48 hours.
3   Drain gherkins, rinse under cold water. Pack gherkins in large sterilised jar; cover completely with spiced vinegar; seal.

SPICED VINEGAR   Combine all ingredients in saucepan, stir over heat, without boiling, until sugar is dissolved. Bring to boil, simmer mixture 2 minutes, stand 5 minutes, strain, cool.

spicy pickled onions

2kg PICKLING ONIONS
780g COARSE COOKING SALT
1.25 LITRES WHITE VINEGAR
1 TABLESPOON COARSE COOKING SALT, EXTRA
1 TABLESPOON SUGAR
1½ TEASPOONS CLOVES
2 TEASPOONS ALLSPICE
2 TEASPOONS BLACK PEPPERCORNS

1   Place unpeeled onions and salt in large bowl, add enough water to just float the onions. Cover; stand 2 days, stirring occasionally. Drain onions, discard liquid. Peel onions carefully, leaving ends intact.
2   Place onions in large heatproof bowl. Cover with boiling water; stand 3 minutes; drain. Repeat this process twice. Pack hot onions firmly into hot sterilised jars.
3   Bring remaining ingredients to a boil in medium saucepan; simmer, uncovered, 15 minutes. Pour hot vinegar mixture over onions in jars to cover completely; seal while hot.

TIP Pickling onions are a very small, brown-skinned variety. Shallots can be substituted if preferred.

TIP After grilling the red peppers, you'll find it easier to peel the skins if you place them in a plastic or paper bag for a few minutes.

pickled peppers

13 SMALL RED PEPPERS (2kg)
1 LITRE WHITE VINEGAR
1 TABLESPOON BLACK PEPPERCORNS
6 SPRIGS FRESH PARSLEY
3 SPRIGS FRESH THYME
2 BAY LEAVES

1 Cut peppers in quarters lengthways, remove seeds. Place peppers, skin-side up, under hot grill. Grill until skin blisters, cool slightly; remove skin. Pack peppers into hot sterilised jars.
2 Combine vinegar, peppercorns and herbs in medium saucepan; bring to a boil. Simmer, uncovered, 5 minutes; strain. Pour hot vinegar over peppers to cover; seal when cold.

spiced vegetable pickles

2 CUCUMBERS (560g), PEELED
½ CAULIFLOWER (1kg), CHOPPED
6 SPRING ONIONS (250G), HALVED
250g GREEN BEANS, CHOPPED
1 RED PEPPER (150g), CHOPPED
2 TABLESPOONS COARSE
COOKING SALT

SPICED VINEGAR
1.5 LITRES WHITE VINEGAR
55g SUGAR
1 TABLESPOON BLACK
PEPPERCORNS
2cm PIECE GINGER, PEELED, SLICED
5 SMALL RED CHILLIES, HALVED
3 BAY LEAVES
2 CLOVES GARLIC, CHOPPED

1 Cut cucumbers in half lengthways, remove seeds: chop the cucumbers coarsely.
2 Combine cucumbers, cauliflower, onions, beans and pepper in large bowl. Sprinkle with salt, cover with boiling water, stand for 10 minutes; drain.
3 Pack vegetables into sterlised jars, cover vegetables completely with spiced vinegar; seal.

SPICED VINEGAR Combine vinegar and sugar in saucepan, stir over heat without boiling, until sugar is dissolved. Tie remaining ingredients in a piece of muslin, add to pan. Bring to boil, cool. Discard muslin bag.

TIP When handling beet-root or red cabbage, wear clean rubber gloves to avoid staining your hands.

home-pickled beetroot

6 MEDIUM BEETROOT (1kg)
220g SUGAR
1 LITRE CIDER VINEGAR
1 SMALL CINNAMON STICK
8 BLACK PEPPERCORNS
4 SMALL DRIED CHILLIES
1 TEASPOON BLACK MUSTARD SEEDS

1 Trim beetroot, leaving 3cm of the stem attached. Wash carefully. Add beetroot to large pan of cold water; boil 45 minutes or until tender. Let cool in the cooking water. Reserve 125ml of the liquid.
2 Rub skin off beetroot; quarter, then place in hot sterilised jars.
3 Combine reserved cooking liquid, sugar, vinegar and remaining ingredients in large pan; stir over heat, without boiling, until sugar is dissolved Bring to a boil. Pour liquid over beetroot and seal while hot.

MAKES ABOUT 2 LITRES (24 PIECES)

pickled red cabbage

1 MEDIUM RED CABBAGE (4kg)
2 TABLESPOONS COARSE COOKING SALT
750ml WHITE VINEGAR
500ml WATER
110g SUGAR
1 TABLESPOON CLOVES
1 CINNAMON STICK
2 TEASPOONS BLACK PEPPERCORNS
¼ TEASPOON GROUND NUTMEG
¼ TEASPOON GROUND GINGER

1 Remove discoloured outer leaves from cabbage, cut cabbage into quarters, remove thick core. Shred cabbage finely, place in large bowl in layers, sprinkling between each layer with the salt, cover, stand overnight.
2 Drain cabbage, rinse under cold water, drain well. Pack cabbage into large sterilised jar.
3 Combine remaining ingredients in large saucepan, bring to boil, cool. Strain vinegar over cabbage in jar to cover completely; seal while hot.

pickled chillies

1kg FRESH RED THAI CHILLIES
8 DRIED BAY LEAVES
1 TABLESPOON BLACK PEPPERCORNS
1 TABLESPOON CORIANDER SEEDS
625ml WATER
55g FINE SEA SALT
1 TABLESPOON SUGAR
375ml WHITE VINEGAR
375ml MALT VINEGAR

1 Add chillies to large saucepan of boiling water; return to boil, drain. Rinse chillies under cold water; drain well. Pack chillies, bay leaves, peppercorns and seeds firmly into hot sterilised jars.
2 Combine the water, salt and sugar in medium pan; stir over heat until salt dissolves and mixture boils. Remove pan from heat, stir in vinegars.
3 Pour vinegar mixture over chillies in jars to cover completely; seal while hot.

MAKES ABOUT 2 LITRES

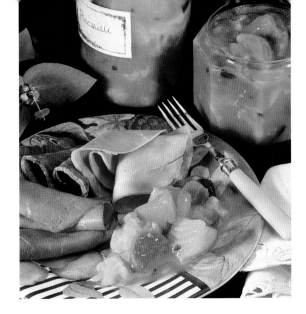

piccalilli

½ SMALL CAULIFLOWER (350g), CHOPPED COARSELY
2 MEDIUM CARROTS (240g), SLICED THINLY
2 TRIMMED CELERY STICKS (150g), SLICED THICKLY
2 SMALL GREEN TOMATOES (260g), CHOPPED COARSELY
1 LARGE CUCUMBER (400g), SLICED THICKLY
10 BABY ONIONS (250g), QUARTERED
260g COARSE COOKING SALT
1.25 LITRES WHITE VINEGAR
220g SUGAR
1 TABLESPOON GROUND TURMERIC
1 TABLESPOON MUSTARD POWDER
½ TEASPOON GROUND GINGER
2 CLOVES GARLIC, CRUSHED
2 RED THAI CHILLIES, DESEEDED, CHOPPED FINELY
35g CORNFLOUR
60ml WHITE VINEGAR, EXTRA

1 Combine cauliflower, carrot, celery, tomato, cucumber, onion and salt in large bowl. Cover; stand overnight.
2 Rinse vegetables under cold water; drain well. Combine vinegar, sugar, turmeric, mustard powder, ginger, garlic and chilli in large saucepan; bring to a boil. Add vegetables; simmer, covered, about 5 minutes or until vegetables are just tender. Stir in blended cornflour and extra vinegar; stir over heat until mixture boils and thickens.
3 Spoon hot piccalilli into hot sterilised jars; seal while hot.

MAKES ABOUT 3 LITRES

pickles

cordials & liqueurs

homemade lemonade

4 MEDIUM LEMONS (560g)
880g CASTER SUGAR
500ml WATER
5 LITRES MINERAL WATER

1 Remove rind from lemons using a vegetable peeler, avoiding white pith; reserve lemons. Combine rind, sugar and the water in large pan; stir over low heat, without boiling, until sugar is dissolved. Bring to a boil, simmer, uncovered, without stirring, about 10 minutes or until syrup is thickened slightly; cool.
2 Squeeze juice from lemons — you will need 250ml lemon juice. Add juice to syrup, strain into jug; cover, keep refrigerated.
3 Just before serving, add four parts mineral water to one part lemonade, or to taste.

MAKES 1.25 LITRES UNDILUTED LEMONADE

orange cordial

6 ORANGES
1 LEMON
375ml WATER
330g SUGAR, APPROXIMATELY

1 Peel rind from oranges and lemon, making sure not to take any pith; this will make the cordial bitter. Squeeze juice from oranges and lemon.
2 Place rind and water in saucepan, bring to boil, reduce heat, simmer gently, covered, 5 minutes. Strain liquid, add to strained orange and lemon juice.
3 Measure liquid in cups, add ½ cup sugar to each cup of liquid. Return to pan, stir over heat until sugar is dissolved; cool, pour into sterilised bottles, seal. Keep refrigerated. Serve diluted with water.

MAKES ABOUT 850ml

■ Cordials are concentrated fruit juices, diluted with chilled water or soda water to make a refreshing drink. The amount of cordial used depends on the strength of flavour preferred, but generally 2 to 3 tablespoons of cordial to a glass, topped up with water, with ice cubes added, is sufficient.

■ Cordials should be stored in the refrigerator and will keep for up to 2 weeks.

lemon barley cordial

6 LEMONS, APPROXIMATELY
(YOU WILL NEED 375ml LEMON
JUICE)
4 TABLESPOONS BARLEY
1 LITRE WATER
880g SUGAR
2 TEASPOONS CITRIC ACID

1 Squeeze juice from lemons. Remove rind, remove any white pith. Put rinds in saucepan with barley and water. Bring to boil, reduce heat, simmer gently uncovered 20 minutes. Add sugar and strained lemon juice, stir until sugar is dissolved, simmer uncovered further 10 minutes. Add citric acid, stir until dissolved
2 Cool, pour into cold sterilised bottles, seal. Keep refrigerated. Serve diluted with water.

MAKES ABOUT 2.5 LITRES

lime cordial

440g SUGAR
250ml WATER
1 EGG WHITE
12 SMALL LIMES, APPROXIMATELY
(YOU WILL NEED 250ml LIME JUICE)

1 Combine sugar, water and unbeaten egg white in saucepan, stir over heat until sugar is dissolved, bring to boil, remove from heat, strain through fine cloth. Add strained lime juice.
2 Cool, pour into cold sterilised bottles, seal. Keep refrigerated. Serve diluted with water.

MAKES ABOUT 750ml

raspberry & cranberry cordial

300g FROZEN RASPBERRIES, THAWED
125ml CRANBERRY JUICE
500ml WATER
220g CASTER SUGAR

1 Blend raspberries and cranberry juice until smooth.
2 Combine water and sugar in medium saucepan, stir over heat, without boiling, until sugar dissolves; bring to a boil. Reduce heat; simmer, without stirring, 5 minutes. Add raspberry mixture to pan; bring to a boil. Reduce heat; simmer, uncovered, 2 minutes.
3 Strain cordial into medium jug, discard seeds; refrigerate 30 minutes. Pour into sterilised bottles, seal. Keep refrigerated. Serve one part cordial mixed to three parts chilled water or soda water.

MAKES ABOUT 750ML

blueberry cordial

330g SUGAR
500ml WATER
250g BLUEBERRIES
2 TEASPOONS TARTARIC ACID

1 Combine sugar and water in a saucepan, stir constantly over heat, without boiling, until sugar is dissolved. Bring to boil, reduce heat, simmer 10 minutes without stirring.
2 Add blueberries, simmer 5 minutes, crush blueberries slightly with wooden spoon to release the colour from the fruit.
3 Blend or process blueberry mixture until smooth, add tartaric acid, strain, discard skins. Cool before bottling in sterilised bottles; seal. Keep refrigerated. Serve diluted with water.

MAKES ABOUT 1 LITRE

cordials & liqueurs

ginger beer soda

250g FRESH GINGER
750ml WATER
440g SUGAR
60ml LEMON JUICE

1 Scrape ginger thoroughly, trim away any bruised parts; chop finely. Place in enamel or stainless steel saucepan with the water, bring to boil, reduce heat, simmer 5 minutes, cover with a cloth, stand overnight.
2 Strain through fine cloth, discard ginger, return liquid to pan with sugar, stir over heat until sugar is dissolved, bring to boil, reduce heat, simmer 5 minutes, add lemon juice. Strain through fine cloth, cool, pour into sterilised bottles, seal. Keep refrigerated.

MAKES ABOUT 750ML

TIP Dilute ginger beer soda with soda water; water does not give the same fresh taste.

TIPS Don't waste the fruit from the liqueur; serve it with cream or ice-cream for a special treat.

■ For a liqueur made with berries, you can use fresh or frozen varieties with equally good results.

brandied orange liqueur

3 LARGE ORANGES (660g)
250ml BRANDY
275g SUGAR
¼ TEASPOON GROUND CORIANDER
¼ TEASPOON GROUND CINNAMON

1 Peel rind thinly from oranges, using vegetable peeler; finely chop rind. Squeeze juice from oranges; you will need 1 cup juice. Combine rind, juice, brandy, sugar, coriander and cinnamon in bowl, cover tightly, stand 2 days; stirring occasionally.
2 Strain mixture through fine cloth, reserve liquid; discard pulp.
3 Pour liquid into sterilised bottle; seal.

MAKES ABOUT 500ml

strawberry liqueur

500g STRAWBERRIES
500ml GIN
1 TABLESPOON GRENADINE SYRUP
165g CASTER SUGAR

1 Hull strawberries, chop roughly. Combine strawberries, gin and grenadine in large bowl, cover, refrigerate 2 days.
2 Add sugar to bowl, stand, uncovered, for about 2 hours or until sugar is dissolved, stirring occasionally. Strain mixture through fine cloth into large jug, reserve liquid; discard pulp.
3 Pour into sterilised bottle; seal.

MAKES ABOUT 750ml

peach citrus liqueur

3 MEDIUM PEACHES (500g), HALVED, PITTED
165g SUGAR
6cm PIECE ORANGE RIND
250ml BRANDY
60ml COINTREAU
1 CINNAMON STICK

1   Chop peaches roughly; combine in large bowl with sugar, rind, brandy, liqueur and cinnamon, cover tightly; refrigerate mixture for 1 week.
2   Strain mixture through fine cloth, pour into sterilised bottle; seal.

MAKES ABOUT 500ml

cherry brandy liqueur

500g CHERRIES, PITTED
220g SUGAR
750ml BRANDY
1 CINNAMON STICK

1   Combine cherries and sugar in large sterilised jar, cover with tight-fitting lid, stand 2 to 3 days; shake jar daily until juice begins to appear.
2   Add brandy and cinnamon to jar, seal tightly, stand 3 months in cool dark place, shaking jar occasionally. Strain cherries through fine cloth, reserve liquid, discard pulp. Pour liquid into sterilised bottles; seal.

MAKES ABOUT 1 LITRE

apricot wine liqueur

12 MEDIUM APRICOTS (500g), HALVED, PITTED
440g SUGAR
1 LITRE DRY WHITE WINE
500ml GIN

1   Combine apricots, sugar and wine in large saucepan. Stir over heat, without boiling, until sugar is dissolved, bring to boil, simmer, covered, 5 minutes; cool. Transfer mixture to large bowl, stir in gin, cover tightly, stand liqueur in a cool dark place for 5 days.
2   Strain mixture through fine cloth, reserve liquid; discard pulp. Pour into sterilised bottles; seal.

MAKES ABOUT 1.75 LITRES

▨ LIQUEURS You can make superb liqueurs by adding fruit to a sweetened spirit base. They must be stored in a cool dark place at all stages of preparation, and must be sealed tightly to prevent evaporation. At some stage in the making, as specified in the recipes, fruit is macerated in the spirit to develop luscious flavour; very little cooking is involved.

▨ Most liqueurs should be kept for at least 6 weeks after bottling. Exceptions are those mixed with fruit and left to stand for a period before bottling, for example, cherry brandy liqueur.

butters & spreads

We like to use unsalted butter where required in these recipes, but regular salted butter works just as well. Most of the butters in this section need to be cooked gently over simmering water. Use either a double saucepan or a large heatproof bowl (glass or china are best) placed over a saucepan of simmering water. The simmering water should not touch the base of the bowl or the base of the top half of the double saucepan. The mixtures must not boil, but will thicken like a custard. The butter in the ingredients will set the butters firmer when cold.

All recipes will keep for several weeks in the refrigerator.

citrus spread

2 LARGE ORANGES (440g)
1 MEDIUM LEMON (180g)
1 MEDIUM LIME (85g)
1 LITRE WATER
1.75kg SUGAR

1 Blend or process unpeeled, chopped fruit, with seeds, with the water in batches until finely chopped.
2 Transfer mixture to large saucepan, add sugar, stir over heat, without boiling, until sugar is dissolved. Bring to boil, boil, uncovered, without stirring, for about 15 minutes or until mixture will spread when cold. Pour into hot sterilised jars; seal when cold.

MAKES ABOUT 2 LITRES

lemon ginger butter

6 EGG YOLKS
165g CASTER SUGAR
1 TEASPOON GRATED LEMON RIND
250ml LEMON JUICE
1½ TEASPOONS GROUND GINGER
3 TABLESPOONS STEM GINGER, FINELY CHOPPED
180g BUTTER, CHOPPED

1 Combine egg yolks and sugar in top half of double saucepan or in heatproof bowl, stir in rind, juice, gingers and butter.
2 Stir over simmering water until mixture thickly coats the back of a wooden spoon.
3 Pour into hot sterilised jars; seal when cold.

MAKES ABOUT 500ml

lemon & lime butter

180g BUTTER, CHOPPED
500ml CASTER SUGAR
125ml LEMON JUICE
1 TEASPOON GRATED LIME RIND
83ml LIME JUICE
4 EGGS, BEATEN, STRAINED

1 Combine all ingredients in top half of double saucepan or in heatproof bowl. Stir over simmering water until mixture thickly coats the back of a wooden spoon.
2 Pour into hot sterilised jars; seal when cold.

MAKES ABOUT 750ml

cherry lemon spread

1.25kg CHERRIES, PITTED
125ml WATER
440g SUGAR, APPROXIMATELY
½ TEASPOON GRATED LEMON RIND
2 TABLESPOONS LEMON JUICE

1 Combine cherries and water in large saucepan, bring to boil, simmer, covered, for about 15 minutes or until cherries are soft. Push cherries through sieve, discard skins. Measure cherry mixture; allow 1 cup sugar to each cup of cherry mixture. Return cherry mixture and sugar to pan, add rind and juice. Stir over heat, without boiling, until sugar is dissolved.
2 Bring to boil, boil, uncovered, for about 15 minutes or until mixture will spread when cold.
3 Pour into hot sterilised jars; seal when cold.

MAKES ABOUT 500ml

orange passionfruit butter

5 EGGS, BEATEN, STRAINED
165g CASTER SUGAR
2 PASSIONFRUIT
3 TEASPOONS GRATED ORANGE RIND
125ml ORANGE JUICE
60ml WATER
125g BUTTER, CHOPPED

1 Combine eggs and sugar in top half of double saucepan or in heatproof bowl. Stir in passionfruit pulp and remaining ingredients.
2 Stir mixture over simmering water until mixture thickly coats the back of a wooden spoon.
3 Pour into hot sterilised jars; seal when cold.

MAKES ABOUT 750ml

butters & spreads

TIP Presented in attractive jars, butters and spreads make welcome gifts at Christmas.

nutty plum spread

14 MEDIUM PLUMS (1kg)
440G BROWN SUGAR
60ml ORANGE JUICE
60ml LEMON JUICE
6 TABLESPOONS CHOPPED PECANS OR WALNUTS
6 TABLESPOONS CHOPPED STEM GINGER

1 Halve plums, discard stones, chop plums roughly. Combine plums, sugar and juices in large saucepan. Stir over heat, without boiling, until sugar is dissolved, bring to boil, simmer, uncovered, stirring occasionally, for about 20 minutes or until mixture is thick and will spread when cold. Stir in nuts and ginger.
2 Pour into hot sterilised jars; seal when cold.

MAKES ABOUT 750ml

plum butter

7 MEDIUM PLUMS (500g), PITTED, CHOPPED
60ml LEMON JUICE
4 EGGS, BEATEN, STRAINED
165g CASTER SUGAR
125g BUTTER, CHOPPED

1 Combine plums and juice in large saucepan. Bring to boil, simmer, covered, for about 20 minutes or until plums are soft. Push plum mixture through sieve. Discard pulp.
2 Combine eggs and sugar in top half of double saucepan or in heatproof bowl; stir in plum mixture and butter. Stir over simmering water until mixture thickly coats the back of a wooden spoon.
3 Pour mixture into hot sterilised jars; seal when cold.

MAKES ABOUT 750ml

raspberry red spread

250g RASPBERRIES
440g CASTER SUGAR
45g CORNFLOUR
2 EGGS, BEATEN, STRAINED
2 TABLESPOONS GRATED LEMON RIND
165ml LEMON JUICE
80g BUTTER, CHOPPED

1 Blend or process berries until smooth. Combine berries and remaining ingredients in saucepan, stir over heat until mixture boils and thickens.
2 Pour mixture into hold sterilised jars; seal when cold.

MAKES ABOUT 750ml

TIP The raspberries in this recipe can be replaced with loganberries, blackberries or strawberries.

butters & spreads

sauces

plum sauce

20 MEDIUM PLUMS (1.5kg), PITTED, CHOPPED
330g BROWN SUGAR
500ml MALT VINEGAR
1 TEASPOON CLOVES
2 CINNAMON STICKS
2 STAR ANISE
5cm PIECE FRESH GINGER, PEELED, BRUISED

1   Combine plums, sugar and vinegar in large pan, stir over heat, without boiling, until sugar dissolves. Tie cloves, cinnamon, star anise and ginger in piece of muslin; add to pan. Bring to boil, simmer, uncovered, stirring occasionally, for 45 minutes or until thick. Discard muslin bag. Pour into hot sterilised jars; seal when cold.

MAKES ABOUT 750ml

The beauty of home-made sauces is that they can be as thick or as thin as you like. Simply cook the mixture until it's about the consistency you want, let a tablespoon of the mixture cool to room temperature. Test the consistency again and cook further if not thick enough.

These sauces should be kept in the refrigerator after they are opened. Be sure to read the tips and techniques on pages 4 to 9 before you start.

spicy sauce

20 MEDIUM RIPE TOMATOES (2kg), CHOPPED
¼ TEASPOON CAYENNE PEPPER
1 MEDIUM ONION (120g), CHOPPED
55g SUGAR
250ml MALT VINEGAR
2 TEASPOONS COARSE COOKING SALT
½ TEASPOON GROUND ALLSPICE
½ TEASPOON GROUND CINNAMON
½ TEASPOON GROUND CLOVES
½ TEASPOON GROUND GINGER

1   Combine tomatoes, pepper, onion and sugar in large saucepan. Bring to boil, simmer, uncovered, stirring occasionally, for about 30 minutes or until thick. Blend or process mixture in batches until smooth. Strain sauce into pan, stir in vinegar, salt and spices. Bring to boil, simmer, uncovered, for 5 minutes.
2   Pour into hot sterilised jars; seal when cold.

MAKES ABOUT 1 LITRE

barbecue sauce

2 TABLESPOONS OIL
2 CLOVES GARLIC, CRUSHED
2 MEDIUM ONIONS (240g), CHOPPED
I SMALL FRESH RED CHILLI, CHOPPED
4 MEDIUM RIPE TOMATOES (400g), CHOPPED
I CELERY STICK, CHOPPED
I LARGE APPLE (200g), CHOPPED
125ml DRY RED WINE
2 TABLESPOONS BROWN SUGAR
I TABLESPOON WHOLEGRAIN MUSTARD
¼ TEASPOON COARSE COOKING SALT
¼ TEASPOON GROUND BLACK PEPPER
I TABLESPOON MALT VINEGAR

I   Heat oil in saucepan, add garlic, onions and chilli, cook until onions are soft. Stir in remaining ingredients, bring to boil, simmer, uncovered, stirring occasionally, for about 30 minutes or until mixture is thick. Blend or process mixture until smooth, push through fine sieve; discard pulp. Pour sauce into hot sterilised jars; seal when cold.

MAKES ABOUT 500ml

worcestershire sauce

750ml MALT VINEGAR
125ml TREACLE
125ml PLUM JAM
I SMALL ONION (75g), CHOPPED
I CLOVE GARLIC, CRUSHED
¼ TEASPOON CHILLI POWDER
I TEASPOON GROUND ALLSPICE
¼ TEASPOON GROUND CLOVES
¼ TEASPOON CAYENNE PEPPER

I   Combine all ingredients in large saucepan. Stir over heat until mixture boils, simmer, uncovered, for I hour, stirring occasionally.
2   Strain mixture into hot sterilised jars; seal when cold.

MAKES ABOUT 500ml

raspberry cider sauce

2kg RASPBERRIES
625ml CIDER VINEGAR
I TEASPOON FRENCH MUSTARD
½ TEASPOON MIXED SPICE
145g SUGAR

I   Combine raspberries and vinegar in large saucepan. Bring to boil, simmer, uncovered, for 15 minutes. Stir in mustard and spice, simmer further 30 minutes. Strain mixture into clean pan through fine sieve; discard seeds. Stir in sugar, stir over heat, without boiling, until sugar is dissolved. Bring to boil, simmer, uncovered, stirring occasionally, for 30 minutes. Pour into hot sterilised jars; seal when cold.

MAKES ABOUT I LITRE

tomato ketchup

1 TEASPOON BLACK PEPPERCORNS
6 WHOLE CLOVES
1 BAY LEAF
8 LARGE TOMATOES (2kg), CHOPPED COARSELY
2 MEDIUM WHITE ONIONS (300g),
CHOPPED COARSELY
125ml RED WINE VINEGAR
220g SUGAR
2 TEASPOONS COARSE COOKING SALT
1 TABLESPOON TOMATO PASTE

1 Tie peppercorns, cloves and bay leaf in piece of muslin. Place muslin bag in large heavy-based saucepan with tomato and onion; bring to a boil. Simmer, uncovered, stirring occasionally, about 45 minutes or until onion is soft. Discard bag. Cool mixture 10 minutes.
2 Blend or process mixture until smooth; strain through fine sieve back into same pan. Add remaining ingredients; stir over heat, without boiling, until sugar dissolves. Simmer, uncovered, stirring occasionally, about 15 minutes or until mixture thickens to desired pouring consistency.
3 Pour hot ketchup into hot sterilised bottles or jars; seal while hot. Store in a cool, dark place for up to 6 months; refrigerate after opening,

MAKES ABOUT 1.25 LITRES

mustard sauce

125ml OIL
3 TABLESPOONS WHITE MUSTARD SEEDS, CRUSHED
4 EGGS
55g SUGAR
1½ TABLESPOONS MUSTARD POWDER
1 TEASPOON COARSE COOKING SALT
½ TEASPOON CRACKED BLACK PEPPERCORNS
2 TEASPOONS PLAIN FLOUR
250ml WHITE VINEGAR

1 Heat oil in pan, add seeds, cook until lightly browned; cool. Blend or process eggs, sugar, mustard powder, salt, peppercorns and flour until smooth. With motor operating, pour in vinegar in a thin stream, then pour in mustard seed mixture in a thin stream.
2 Transfer mixture to pan, stir over heat until mixture boils and thickens slightly. Pour sauce into hot sterilised jars; seal when cold.

MAKES ABOUT 500ml

tomato & chilli sauce

3 CLOVES GARLIC
1½ TABLESPOONS PIMENTOS
3 TEASPOONS CLOVES
2 TEASPOONS BLACK PEPPERCORNS
15 MEDIUM RIPE TOMATOES (1.5kg), PEELED, CHOPPED
330g SUGAR
165ml WHITE VINEGAR
2 TEASPOONS COARSE COOKING SALT
3 MEDIUM FRESH RED CHILLIES, CHOPPED

1 Tie garlic, pimentos, cloves and peppercorns in piece of muslin. Combine remaining ingredients with muslin bag in large saucepan, stir over heat, without boiling until sugar is dissolved.
2 Bring to boil, simmer, uncovered, stirring occasionally, for about 45 minutes or until mixture thickens slightly. Discard muslin bag. Blend or process mixture in several batches until smooth. Pour sauce into hot sterilised jars; seal when cold.

MAKES ABOUT 750ml

sauces

glossary

ALLSPICE also known as pimento or jamaican pepper; so-named because it tastes like a combination of nutmeg, cumin, clove and cinnamon – all spices.

ALMONDS flat, pointy ended nuts with pitted **brown** shell enclosing a creamy white kernel that is covered by a brown skin.

slivered cut lengthways.

AMARETTO an almond-flavoured liqueur.

AUBERGINE also known as eggplant.

baby small, finger-shaped aubergine with dark-purple glossy skin.

BEETROOT also known as beets.

CARDAMOM seeds native to India and used extensively in its cuisine; can be purchased in pod, seed or ground form. Has an aromatic, sweetly rich flavour and is one of the world's most expensive spices.

CAYENNE PEPPER thin-fleshed, long, very-hot red chilli; usually purchased dried and ground.

CERTO commercially-made pectin product extracted from apples; used in the home jam making process.

CHILLI available in many different types and sizes. Use rubber gloves when deseeding and chopping fresh chillies as they can burn your skin. Removing seeds and membranes lessens the heat level.

powder crushed dried chillies blended to a powder.

thai small, medium-to-hot chilli that ranges from bright-red to dark-green in colour.

CINNAMON STICK dried inner bark of the shoots of the cinnamon tree; also available in ground form.

CITRIC ACID commonly found in most fruits, especially limes and lemons. Commercial citric acid helps accentuate the acid flavour of fruit; it does not act as a preservative.

CLOVES can be used whole or in ground form. Has a strong scent and taste so should be used minimally.

COCONUT, FLAKED flaked and dried coconut flesh.

COINTREAU citrus-flavoured liqueur.

CORIANDER dried a fragrant herb; coriander seeds and ground coriander must never be used to replace fresh coriander or vice versa. The tastes are completely different.

CORNFLOUR also known as cornstarch; used as a thickening agent in cooking.

CUMIN SEEDS aromatic and nutty, cumin seeds are the dried fruit of a plant from the parsley family; also available in ground form.

CURRY POWDER a blend of ground spices; choose mild or hot to suit your taste and the recipe.

DATES fruit from the date palm; have brown paper-thin skin and sticky, sweet flesh with a long seed. Available fresh or dried (pitted or with stones).

FIVE-SPICE a fragrant mixture of ground cinnamon, cloves, star anise, Sichuan pepper and fennel seeds.

FOOD COLOURINGS available in liquid, powdered and concentrated paste forms.

FRAMBOISE a raspberry-flavoured liqueur; crème de framboises is sweeter.

GARAM MASALA a blend of spices based on varying proportions of cardamom, cinnamon, cloves, coriander, fennel and cumin, roasted and ground together. Black pepper and chilli can be added for a hotter version.

GHERKIN miniature cucumber.

GINGER

fresh also called green or root ginger; the thick gnarled root of a tropical plant. Can be kept, peeled, covered with dry sherry in a jar and refrigerated, or frozen in an airtight container.

stem fresh ginger that has been crystallised in sugar syrup.

GRAND MARNIER orange-flavoured liqueur based on Cognac-brandy.

GRAPEFRUIT large, yellow-skinned citrus fruit; has tart flavour.

GRENADINE SYRUP non-alcoholic flavouring made from pomegranate juice; bright red in colour. Imitation cordial is also available.

KIRSCH cherry-flavoured liqueur. kiwi fruit also known as Chinese gooseberry.

LIQUID SWEETENER an artificial no-calorie sweetener; available from supermarkets.

MIXED SPICE a blend of ground spices usually consisting of cinnamon, allspice and nutmeg.

MUSTARD

dijon a pale brown, distinctively flavoured, fairly mild French mustard.

french plain mild mustard.

powder finely ground mustard seeds. mustard seeds, black and yellow: acrid seeds from any of several species of mustard plants; used for pickling, as a seasoning in savoury dishes, to make freshly ground mustard, and as an ingredient in salad dressings.

wholegrain also known as seeded; a French-style coarse-grain mustard made from crushed mustard seeds and Dijon-style French mustard.

NUTMEG dried nut of an evergreen tree; available in ground form or you can grate your own with a fine grater.

OIL

groundnut made from ground peanuts, groundnut oil has a high smoking point; the most commonly used oil in Asian cooking.

olive mono-unsaturated oil made from the pressing of tree-ripened olives.

vegetable any of a number of oils sourced from plants rather than animal fats.

ONION

red also known as Spanish, red Spanish or Bermuda onion; a sweet-flavoured, large, purple-red onion that is particularly good eaten raw in salads.

pickling a very small, brown-skinned variety. Shallots can be substituted if preferred.

ORANGE, SEVILLE orange variety that is very tart in flavour; suitable only for jam-making.

PAPAYA also known as pawpaw; thin-skinned tropical fruit, the ripe flesh of which varies from orange to yellow to pink in colour. Green pawpaw is a popular ingredient in curries and chutney.

PAPRIKA ground dried red bell pepper (capsicum); available sweet or hot.

PASSIONFRUIT also known as granadilla; a small tropical fruit, native to Brazil, comprised of a tough skin surrounding edible black sweet-sour seeds.

PEPPER also known as bell pepper or capsicum.

PINE NUTS also known as pignoli; small, cream-coloured kernels obtained from the cones of different varieties of pine trees.

PORT sweet fortified wine with alcohol content of 18% to 20%.

QUINCE large, yellow-skinned, fragrant fruit with crunchy cream flesh that, when slow-cooked, turns a deep ruby-red in colour.

RHUBARB vegetable (though eaten as a fruit) with cherry-red stalks and green leaves. The stalks are the only edible part of rhubarb; the leaves contain oxalic acid and are toxic.

ROSÉ WINE slightly sweet wine with pale-pink colour; made from dark grapes.

RUM liquor made from fermented sugarcane.

SAUTERNES a sweet white wine made from late-harvested premium grapes; often referred to as a botrytis or sticky wine.

SHERRY, SWEET sweet fortified wine originally from the south of Spain.

STAR ANISE a dried star-shaped pod, the seeds of which taste of aniseed.

SUGAR we used coarse, granulated table sugar, also known as crystal sugar, unless otherwise specified.

brown an extremely soft, finely granulated sugar retaining molasses for its characteristic colour and flavour.

caster also known as superfine or finely granulated table sugar.

palm: very fine sugar from the coconut palm. It is sold in cakes, and is also known as gula jawa, gula melaka and jaggery. Palm sugar can be replaced with brown or black sugar.

raw natural brown granulated sugar.

TAMARIND

concentrate thick paste made from the acid-tasting fruit of the tamarind tree. To dilute, follow instructions on packet.

dried the reddish-brown pulp, stones, rind and roots of the bean of the tamarind tree. To extract its acidic, sour essence, soak in boiling water until cool then press though a sieve back into the soaking water; use the flavoured water and discard the pulp.

TARTARIC ACID is used in making sweets and preserves to prevent the crystallisation of the sugar.

TOMATO

green medium-sized tomato with piquant flavour; well suited to relishes.

paste triple-concentrated tomato puree used to flavour soups, stews and sauces.

TREACLE thick, dark syrup not unlike molasses; a by-product from sugar refining.

TURMERIC a member of the ginger family, its root is dried and ground; intensely pungent in taste but not hot.

VINEGAR

balsamic authentic only from the province of Modena, Italy; made from wine of white Trebbiano grapes and aged in antique wooden casks.

cider made from fermented apples.

malt made from fermented malted barley and beech shavings.

red wine based on fermented red wine.

white made from spirit of cane sugar.

white wine made from fermented white wine.

WHISKY we used a good quality Scotch whisky.

WINE, SWEET WHITE we used a moselle wine.

index

conversion charts

MEASURES

■ The spoon measurements used in this book are metric: one metric tablespoon holds 20ml; one metric teaspoon holds 5ml.

■ All spoon measurements are level.

■ The most accurate way of measuring dry ingredients is to weigh them.

■ When measuring liquids, use a clear glass or plastic jug with metric markings.

■ We use large eggs with an average weight of 60g.

DRY MEASURES

metric	imperial
15g	1/2oz
30g	1oz
60g	2oz
90g	3oz
125g	4oz (1/4lb)
155g	5oz
185g	6oz
220g	7oz
250g	8oz (1/2lb)
280g	9oz
315g	10oz
345g	11oz
375g	12oz (3/4lb)
410g	13oz
440g	14oz
470g	15oz
500g	16oz (1lb)
750g	24oz (1 1/2lb)
1kg	32oz (2lb)

LIQUID MEASURES

metric	imperial
30ml	1 fl oz
60ml	2 fl oz
100ml	3 fl oz
125ml	4 fl oz
150ml	5 fl oz (1/4 pint/1 gill)
190ml	6 fl oz
250ml	8 fl oz
300ml	10 fl oz (1/2 pt)
500ml	16 fl oz
600ml	20 fl oz (1 pint)
1000ml (1 litre)	1 3/4 pints

LENGTH MEASURES

metric	imperial
3mm	1/8in
6mm	1/4in
1cm	1/2in
2cm	3/4in
2.5cm	1in
5cm	2in
6cm	2 1/2in
8cm	3in
10cm	4in
13cm	5in
15cm	6in
18cm	7in
20cm	8in
23cm	9in
25cm	10in
28cm	11in
30cm	12in (1ft)

OVEN TEMPERATURES

These oven temperatures are only a guide for conventional ovens. For fan-assisted ovens, check the manufacturer's manual.

	°C (Celcius)	°F (Fahrenheit)	gas mark
Very low	120	250	1/2
Low	150	275-300	1-2
Moderately low	170	325	3
Moderate	180	350-375	4-5
Moderately hot	200	400	6
Hot	220	425-450	7-8
Very hot	240	475	9